I0031216

Vicarious Liability in the Sports Industry

This timely book is the first to critically examine the doctrine of vicarious liability in the context of the sports industry.

Drawing on theoretical, empirical and interdisciplinary research, the book focuses on the close connection test at stage two of vicarious liability, highlighting how vicarious liability could be used to hold sports employers strictly liable for a wide range of on-the-field and off-the-field harms committed by their athletes. It considers the extent to which vicarious liability might be applied to clubs and sporting organisations for personal injuries and racial abuse suffered by participants during competition, and examines whether employers in the sports industry ought to be held vicariously liable for the sexual assault of young athletes and women away from the field.

This book is important reading for any student, researcher or practitioner interested in sports law, tort law, private law theory, socio-legal studies, jurisprudence, gender studies and sports ethics.

James Brown is a Lecturer in Law at Manchester Law School, Manchester Metropolitan University, UK. His research interests lie in the areas of sports law, tort law and private law theory, and he has published several articles on these issues. James holds a PhD in Law from the University of Sheffield and an LLM (with Distinction) in Sports Law from Nottingham Trent University.

Ethics and Sport
Series editors
Mike McNamee, *University of Wales, Swansea*
Jim Parry, *Charles University, Prague, Czech Republic*

The *Ethics and Sport* series aims to encourage critical reflection on the practice of sport, and to stimulate professional evaluation and development. Each volume explores new work relating to philosophical ethics and the social and cultural study of ethical issues. Each is different in scope, appeal, focus and treatment but a balance is sought between local and international focus, perennial and contemporary issues, level of audience, teaching and research application, and variety of practical concerns.

Titles in the series:

For more information about this series, please visit: https://www.routledge.com/Ethics-and-Sport/book-series/EANDS

Vicarious Liability in the Sports Industry

James Brown

Routledge
Taylor & Francis Group

LONDON AND NEW YORK

First published 2024
by Routledge
4 Park Square, Milton Park, Abingdon, Oxon OX14 4RN

and by Routledge
605 Third Avenue, New York, NY 10158

Routledge is an imprint of the Taylor & Francis Group, an informa business

British Library Cataloguing-in-Publication Data
A catalogue record for this book is available from the British Library

Library of Congress Cataloging-in-Publication Data
Names: Brown, James (Lecturer in law), author.
Title: Vicarious liability in the sports industry / James Brown.
Description: Abingdon, Oxon [UK] ; New York, NY : Routledge, 2024. |
Series: Ethics and sport | Includes bibliographical references and index. |
Identifiers: LCCN 2024014643 (print) | LCCN 2024014644 (ebook) |
Subjects: LCSH: Sports—Law and legislation. | Sports—Law and
legislation—Criminal provisions. | Liability (Law) | Personal injuries.
| Racism in sports. Classification: LCC K3702 .B77 2024 (print) |
LCC K3702 (ebook) | DDC 344/.099—dc23/eng/20240409
LC record available at https://lccn.loc.gov/2024014643
LC ebook record available at https://lccn.loc.gov/2024014644

ISBN: 978-1-032-66584-9 (hbk)
ISBN: 978-1-032-66586-3 (pbk)
ISBN: 978-1-032-66587-0 (ebk)

DOI: 10.4324/9781032665870

Typeset in Times New Roman
by codeMantra

Contents

Acknowledgements

Much of the analysis in this book is informed by research that was undertaken for my PhD thesis, which was completed at the University of Sheffield in 2023. As such, I would like to thank the University of Sheffield for funding this project and providing the opportunity for me to undertake the research on this topic. Additionally, I am also greatly indebted to the supervisors of my thesis, Professor Tsachi Keren-Paz and Professor Andreas Rühmkorf. Their wisdom and clarity of thought throughout the writing of my thesis were invaluable, and I am extremely grateful for their support and guidance, which continues to this day.

Further thanks must also go to Professor Mark James, Professor Paula Giliker, Dr David Benbow, Dr Joe Atkinson, Dr Thomas Bennett and Jamie Atkinson for their helpful suggestions and insightful comments on earlier drafts of this work. Additionally, and given that some material from this book was presented at the annual conference of the Socio-Legal Studies Association at Ulster University in April 2023, I am also grateful to the participants of that conference for their helpful comments.

Thanks are also due to the team at Routledge for helping bring this book to publication. In particular, I would like to thank Professor Jim Parry, Professor Mike McNamee and Simon Whitmore. The editorial assistance provided by Rebecca Connor was also very useful.

Finally, I would like to thank my parents for their endless support and encouragement, as well as my partner, Rosie, for her continuous love, patience and generosity.

Acronyms and abbreviations

CAS	Court of Arbitration for Sport
CLS	Critical Legal Studies
CRT	Critical Race Theory
DCMS	Digital, Culture, Media and Sport
EA	Equality Act
FA	Football Association
FIFA	Fédération Internationale de Football Association
MLB	Major League Baseball
NBA	National Basketball Association
NCAA	National Collegiate Athletic Association
NFL	National Football League
NHL	National Hockey League
NRL	National Rugby League
PHA	Protection from Harassment Act
RFU	Rugby Football Union
YCCC	Yorkshire County Cricket Club

1   Introduction

When the prominent American football coach Vince Lombardi remarked that running a football team was 'no different than running any other kind of organisation',[1] it was highly unlikely that he had the law on vicarious liability in mind. However, just as with any enterprise that employs or utilises the services of another, sports clubs run the risk of being held liable for a wide variety of on-the-field and off-the-field acts. The doctrine of vicarious liability is one that is entrenched in the law of tort, and it stands for the proposition that one party (usually an employer) will be strictly liable for the tortious behaviour of another (usually an employee), so long as there is a close connection between the harm and the wrongdoer's relationship with the defendant. For instance, in the sporting context, vicarious liability has previously been employed to hold clubs strictly liable for injuries caused by dangerous tackles and off-the-ball melees on the field of play. Likewise, where it can be established that the tortfeasor acted within the course of their employment, vicarious liability could also be utilised to hold sports employers strictly liable for a variety of off-the-field sexual offences committed by their employees. Liability in such circumstances is imposed on the employer not because they were at fault for the harm but rather because of their relationship with the wrongdoer.

In this regard, it is worth noting that the concept of liability for the actions of another is certainly not a new phenomenon. In fact, it appears to possess its roots in Roman law, and in particular, the notion that the head of the family (the paterfamilias) ought to be responsible for the delicts of their children and slaves.[2] Today, the doctrine of vicarious liability is most commonly used to hold large-scale (oftentimes global) institutions responsible for harm that is intrinsically linked to their enterprise. This was an inevitable by-product of the commercial and industrial developments that occurred in the seventeenth century, as well as the rise in corporate power that materialised as a result of the nineteenth-century Industrial Revolution.[3]

DOI: 10.4324/9781032665870-1

Setting the Ground: Why Assess Vicarious Liability in Sport?

Despite having a long-standing history dating back to medieval times, scholars have yet to identify a coherent theoretical rationale that is able to fully explain the many contours of vicarious liability. It is this omission that informs the two contributions that this book strives to make. First, I explore (from both a descriptive and normative stance) the scope of vicarious liability in the sports industry. As part of this enquiry, I examine how the various theoretical rationales that underpin vicarious liability might be applied to the largely unexplored terrain of the sports industry. The second contribution made by this book is that it assesses what broader lessons we might learn about vicarious liability by applying it to the sporting sector. Ultimately, a sport-specific application of the doctrine highlights that a contextual, theoretical and interdisciplinary approach to vicarious liability is likely to lead to more normatively attractive results in practice. With this in mind, we might ask the following questions: why focus on vicarious liability? And why focus on sport? In answering these questions, it is hoped that I can shed some further light on the significance of this book.

Why Vicarious Liability?

The law on vicarious liability has generated an unprecedented amount of judicial activity in recent years. This may be because, as various scholars have opined, it is an area of law that is 'muddled doctrinally' and 'desperately in need of reform and rationalisation'.[4] As Gray further elucidates, 'the Achilles heel [of vicarious liability] has been the long-running failure of courts and academics to satisfactorily rationalise and justify the imposition of such liability'.[5] At least until the 2020 Supreme Court decisions in *Barclays Bank v Various Claimants*[6] and *WM Morrison Supermarkets v Various Claimants*,[7] the raging debate on the appropriate scope of the doctrine has largely – if not exclusively – been centred around the application of the various theoretical rationales for the doctrine. Much of this discussion stems from the judgment of Lord Phillips in *Various Claimants v Catholic Child Welfare Society*, a case that perhaps marks the zenith of the explicit articulation of theoretical principles in the law on vicarious liability. Here, his Lordship set out five 'policy reasons' that make it 'fair, just and reasonable to impose vicarious liability' on an employer:

> (i) the employer is more likely to have the means to compensate the victim than the employee and can be expected to have insured against that liability; (ii) the tort will have been committed as a result of activity being taken by the employee on behalf of the employer; (iii) the employee's activity is likely to be part of the business activity of the employer; (iv) the employer,

by employing the employee to carry on the activity will have created the risk of the tort committed by the employee; (v) the employee will, to a greater or lesser degree, have been under the control of the employer.[8]

This passage neatly summarises the main theoretical rationales that have long been employed when attempting to explain the existence of vicarious liability. Point (i) encapsulates the theories of deep pockets and loss spreading, whilst points (ii)–(iv) deal with the important notion of enterprise liability. Point (v) captures the idea that employers ought to be vicariously liable because they can control the conduct of their employees. To this, we might also add the deterrence rationale, which suggests that the possibility of vicarious liability provides an incentive for employers to prevent their employees from causing harm.

Whilst many scholars, including myself, have critiqued the notion that vicarious liability can be explained by one solitary theory,[9] enterprise liability seems to have emerged in recent case law as the dominant justification for vicarious liability,[10] and it is for such reasons that the analysis in this book focusses rather extensively on this rationale. Notably, enterprise liability tends to be depicted in two different forms. The first, which is based on the principle of fairness, suggests that if an employer seeks to benefit from engaging in a particular activity, then it is only fair that they equally bear the burden by providing compensation for any loss caused by such activity.[11] The second is concerned with the causal creation of risk, and it suggests that an employer should accept responsibility for any risks which are said to be 'inextricably interwoven' with their enterprise.[12] These two formulations of enterprise liability emanate from the broader principle of distributive justice, which is concerned with the fair distribution of benefits and burdens in society. Unlike corrective justice, it looks past the immediate needs of the two parties in a transaction.[13] As such, and with an enterprise liability-based approach in mind, this book follows in the footsteps of those scholars who adopt a contextual and pluralistic approach to distributive justice.[14]

I have considered elsewhere the benefits of adopting a theoretical approach to vicarious liability,[15] and I will not restate those arguments here. However, besides these points, there are several other reasons for adopting an overtly theoretical methodology in this book. First, it is contended that a sport-specific application of vicarious liability may be able to provide some semblance of clarity to the eclectic array of theories that underpin the doctrine. For instance, later chapters demonstrate that many of these theoretical rationales can be intellectually enriched by adopting an interdisciplinary approach.[16] Additionally, the application of vicarious liability to sport also nicely illustrates how certain theories ought to overlap and interact with each other.[17]

Second, the global appeal of these theoretical rationales means that the analysis in this book is likely to appeal to a wide range of international audiences. Cappelletti has recently compared, for instance, the importance of justifications for strict liability across various common law and civil law jurisdictions, and it is evident that rationales such as enterprise liability, control and loss spreading feature even more prominently in countries such as the US, France and Italy.[18]

Third, the strong emphasis on theory in this book ties in nicely with my preference for a socio-legal conception of the law, and this is reflected in my support for legal realism and empiricism in later chapters. In this light, whilst I intend, of course, to contribute to the current scholarship on vicarious liability, it must be recognised that the analysis in this book is also fundamentally concerned with *what* the purpose of the law is, and *how* judges apply it. As such, much of the discussion may also have wider implications for the use of theory in other areas of law, such as private law (and beyond).

Finally, it is perhaps also worth briefly mentioning how this book contributes to the growing scholarly debate on the importance of theory to vicarious liability. In contrast to some of the leading scholars in this area of law,[19] this work rejects the so-called incremental approach that was emphasised in cases such as *Barclays* and *Morrison*, and it calls for a more consistent and comprehensive analysis of theory than is evident in the current case law. Many commentators appear to suggest that, prior to the Supreme Court judgments in *Barclays* and *Morrison*, the doctrine of vicarious liability had spiralled out of control.[20] In this light, a call was made for a more cautious and principled approach in order to respond to the concern that the doctrine was 'on the move'.[21] One of the purposes of this book is to challenge this retreat and to highlight that a continued expansion of the doctrine is both defensible and normatively desirable.

Importantly, such an expansion may still be possible even in the aftermath of *Barclays* and *Morrison*. After all, by arguing that reference to the underlying rationales of vicarious liability is still permissible in 'doubtful' cases,[22] the Supreme Court in *Barclays* may have left the door open for theory to continue influencing the way that cases are decided in this area of law. This is reinforced by the fact that judges in later cases have continued to refer to theory as a 'final check' on the outcome of a case.[23] Consequently, there is arguably ample scope for a judge to refer to the theoretical arguments outlined in this book when assessing the appropriate scope of vicarious liability in the sports industry.

Why Sport?

With respect to the 'why sport' question, the answer is perhaps less obvious. One might question, for instance, why I did not decide to focus on any other industry in which the principles of vicarious liability might similarly be applicable. The response is two-fold and can be answered from both a narrow and broad perspective. From the narrow point of view, it is evident that the sports sector contains several divergent contexts and scenarios, ranging from, for instance, on-the-field to off-the-field harms and personal to non-personal injuries. Consequently, it is an industry that provides plenty of scope for assessing how a more theoretical, empirical, socio-legal and interdisciplinary law on vicarious liability might work in practice. Given that it is equally a global enterprise watched and played in every corner of the world, a focus on sport also provides ample opportunity to demonstrate the international significance of this analysis (which is reinforced, of course, by the fact that the underlying theories of vicarious liability are of ubiquitous appeal).

Furthermore, it must be noted that there has been very little scholarly work on the scope of vicarious liability in sport, so this book will be the first to provide an in-depth analysis of this issue. Whilst the topic has been sporadically touched upon by some commentators, the treatment that it has received is either not comprehensive enough,[24] lacking in theoretical rigour[25] or outdated in light of developments in the law.[26] In some instances, it is a case of all three.[27] Even the most recent – and arguably the most thorough – examination of sporting vicarious liability by Morgan focusses only on one sport, and it appears to skirt over numerous theoretical justifications and important issues (such as, for instance, the potential liability of clubs for on-field discrimination).[28] As such, this work attempts to fill in this gap, and it aims to demonstrate how some of the theoretical and socio-legal analysis in this book can be translated into concrete practical guidance. Consequently, whilst the discussion here will be of obvious interest to those involved in sports law and tort law, the conclusions formulated in this study may also be of wider appeal to scholars, practitioners (including judges) and students interested in private law theory, jurisprudence, law and society, sports ethics, sports sociology, sports philosophy and gender studies.

Moreover, there may also be an additional broader justification for my focus on sport in this book. In particular, it is hoped that the analysis here will help to contribute to, and advance knowledge in, the emerging area of sports law. Whilst Anderson's claim about the 'under-theorisation' of sports law is perhaps now a less convincing one in light of the growing significance of this field of study,[29] it remains the case that sport has yet to be subjected to any sustained theoretical analysis from a private law perspective. This is the first work to seriously explore this issue,[30] and it is suggested that the discussion in this book may provide a number of important pragmatic and theoretical benefits for the growing area of scholarship related to sports torts.

Scope

Whilst the analysis in this book has widespread theoretical and practical appeal, it is worth highlighting several clarificatory points about the parameters of this work. The first, and perhaps most notable, point is that the book focusses solely on the second stage of vicarious liability. Although the establishment of a sufficient relationship between the tortfeasor and defendant is an important issue to be considered at the first stage of vicarious liability, the focus here will be on identifying a close connection between the wrongdoer's relationship with the defendant and the resulting injury.[31] As Giliker has recently opined, the close connection (or course of employment) test is 'fundamental to our understanding of the doctrine of vicarious liability' because it 'determines the breadth of this strict liability doctrine'.[32] It is perhaps for such reasons that other scholars have also written exclusively about the second limb of vicarious liability.[33] Those seeking to explore various issues relating to the first stage of vicarious liability in sport – such as whether governing bodies and competition organisers could be held strictly liable,[34] who ought to bear responsibility when an athlete is sent out on loan[35] and whether amateur teams could also be held vicariously liable[36] – may wish to consult my earlier work.

The second point of clarification is that this book is limited to vicarious liability for the actions of *athletes*. Now, this is not to say that liability for other parties in the sports industry – such as referees, managers, coaches, medical staff, nutritionists, scouts, etc. – is an insignificant issue. Indeed, recent case law such as *Blackpool Football Club Ltd v DSN* and *TVZ & others v Manchester City Football Club Ltd* illustrates that vicarious liability for scouts and coaches is very much a live issue.[37] However, for purposes of brevity, the focus here will solely be on athletes. Nevertheless, it may be that the discussion in the following chapters provokes a more theoretically nuanced discussion of vicarious liability for those individuals who are part of a club's 'extended family',[38] as it is suggested in Chapter 6 that this is an area ripe for greater socio-legal research.

Third, and in contrast to Morgan's work on this topic, this book endeavours to incorporate analysis of a wide variety of sports. Whilst I do, of course, regularly draw upon insights from the most popular and so-called 'national game' of football,[39] it would be a disservice to my contextualised approach to vicarious liability to focus entirely on this sport. As such, whilst I often use the terms 'on-the-field' and 'off-the-field' throughout this work, these should not be read as limited to those games played on grass. They also include, for instance, sports such as basketball and ice hockey.

Fourth, and relatedly, it may be that the analysis in this book is oftentimes somewhat eclectic, in that it draws upon a diverse array of different legal issues in numerous sports. However, given the various factual nuances in each type of sport – which, as we must remember, is played at numerous levels of expertise – it would perhaps be rather artificial to attempt to present the work in a more holistic manner. This only serves to further reinforce, however, the necessarily contextual and fact-sensitive approach to vicarious liability that is advocated in this book.

Fifth, and on a similar note, I also liberally refer to (and apply) case law from several jurisdictions outside of the UK, such as Canada, Australia and the US. This is, as we have discussed, primarily because the theories of vicarious liability that underpin the doctrine possess universal appeal but also because case law from such jurisdictions (and in particular Canada) have been influential in determining the appropriate scope of the doctrine in the UK. As such, the analysis in this book may be of interest to some comparative law scholars.

Sixth, and finally, it is worth noting that the primary focus here is on vicarious liability in tort. That said, in Chapter 3, I do briefly discuss the relevance of statutory vicarious liability in responding to racist on-the-field slurs used by athletes. Although these two forms of vicarious liability ought to be kept separate, it is surely 'not inconceivable that innovations in statutory interpretation... can also have an influence on the development of the common law, just as the common law plainly influences to some degree the interpretation of the statute'.[40]

Structure

Thematically, the book is divided into two main parts. The first part (Chapters 2 and 3) assesses how the close connection test for vicarious liability might be applied to acts committed *on* the sports field. Accordingly, Chapter 2 deals with the appropriate scope of vicarious liability for personal injuries suffered on the pitch. It provides an in-depth theoretical examination of the only UK case to focus extensively on vicarious liability for on-the-field personal injury: *Gravil v Carroll and Redruth Rugby Football Club*.[41] Despite the Court of Appeal employing both a deterrence and enterprise risk rationale to justify the liability of the semi-professional rugby club in this case, I argue here that the concept of deterrence, whilst still relevant, perhaps ought to be subsidiary to the notion of enterprise liability in this context. In this regard, I assess how an empirical analysis of the risk-related formulation of enterprise liability may help us to avoid a potential clash with the (necessary) assessment of a sport's so-called playing culture at the standard of care stage.

Thereafter, in Chapter 3, I explore whether sports clubs ought to also be held vicariously liable for discriminatory remarks made by their players on the field. The focus in this chapter is on racial discrimination, and I explore how the institutionally racist nature of many sporting organisations could inform an analysis of the close connection test in this context. Critical Race Theory is employed here to buttress an enterprise risk-based approach to race-related harm, and this serves to reinforce the contention that an interdisciplinary model of vicarious liability may be able to produce more normatively desirable results in practice. Finally, the chapter highlights that the current legal options that could be used to hold a club vicariously liable for on-the-field racist behaviour are inadequate. Consequently, in order to remedy this gap in the law, I argue that we should introduce a new (potentially sport-specific) tort of hate speech to combat such harm.

The second part of this book (Chapters 4 and 5) considers the appropriate scope of the close connection test for harmful acts committed by players *off* the field. The focus here is largely on sexual abuse committed by athletes. With one eye on the importance of the closely related areas of law on privacy and unfair dismissal, Chapter 4 outlines how certain sexual offences – such as harm caused during initiation rituals and hazing, as well as the sexual abuse of women away from the locker room – might be said to be an intrinsic risk of many professional sports. Insight is gleaned from interdisciplinary fields of study such as feminist theory and masculinities studies, and this chapter highlights that it may be empirically and normatively appropriate to conclude that one's employment as a professional athlete makes a material contribution to their off-the-field sexual harm.

Lastly, in Chapter 5, I assess how the somewhat unique role model and celebrity status of professional athletes may provide a further fairness justification for imposing vicarious liability in this context. This is based on an assessment of so-called 'disrepute clauses' that are now prevalent in many professional sporting contracts. Given that sports clubs often seek to benefit from an athlete's fame and success by relying on these overly intrusive contractual provisions, it is only fair for them to also bear the burden of any foreseeable risks when an athlete commits harm away from the field. With this analysis in mind, the chapter concludes by outlining six guiding considerations that judges may want to weigh up in deciding whether or not to impose vicarious liability for various off-the-field harms. This guidance once again reaffirms the overtly contextual, theoretical and fact-sensitive nature of my suggested model of vicarious liability.

Notes

1 Family of Vince Lombardi c/o Luminary Group, 'Famous Quotes by Vince Lombardi' <http://www.vincelombardi.com/quotes.html>.
2 Reinhard Zimmermann, *The Law of Obligations: Roman Foundations of the Civilian Tradition* (Clarendon Press 1996) 1118; *Sweeney v Boylan Nominees Pty Ltd* (2006) 226 CLR 161, 169–70.
3 See, e.g., Paula Giliker, *Vicarious Liability in Tort: A Comparative Perspective* (CUP 2010) 6–13.
4 Giliker (n 3) 13; Nicholas McBride and Roderick Bagshaw, *Tort Law* (6th edn, Pearson 2018) 856.
5 Anthony Gray, *Vicarious Liability: Critique and Reform* (Hart 2018) 269.
6 [2020] UKSC 13.
7 [2020] UKSC 12.
8 [2012] UKSC 56, [35].
9 See, e.g., Marco Cappelletti, 'A Pluralist View of Vicarious Liability in Tort' (2024) 140 LQR 61; James Brown, 'Developing a Contextual-pluralist Model of Vicarious

Liability' (2021) 28 Tort L Rev 123; Jason Neyers, 'A Theory of Vicarious Liability' (2005) 43 Alta L Rev 287.

10 *Trustees of the Barry Congregation of Jehovah's Witnesses v BXB* [2023] UKSC 15, [58] (Lord Burrows); *Armes v Nottinghamshire County Council* [2017] UKSC 60, [67] (Lord Reed). See also Paula Giliker, 'Comparative Law and Legal Culture: Placing Vicarious Liability in Comparative Perspective' (2018) 6 CJCL 265, 290.

11 John Fleming, *The Law of Torts* (9th edn, LBC information Services 1998) 410; *Broom v Morgan* [1953] 1 QB 597, 608 (Denning LJ).

12 *Lister v Hesley Hall Ltd* [2002] 1 AC 215, [28] (Lord Steyn).

13 Aristotle, *Nichomachean Ethics Book V* (trans. Martin Ostwald, Bobbs-Merrill 1962), 117–20.

14 Tsachi Keren-Paz, *Torts, Egalitarianism and Distributive Justice* (Ashgate 2007) 15; Hanoch Sheinman, 'Tort Law and Distributive Justice' in John Oberdiek (ed), *Philosophical Foundations of the Law of Torts* (OUP 2014).

15 Brown (n 9) (arguing that a 'thick' approach to theory will lead to a more meaningful, adaptable and transparent law on vicarious liability).

16 See, e.g., the relevance of playing culture (Chapter 2); Critical Race Theory (Chapter 3); and gender studies (Chapters 4 and 5) to the enterprise liability rationale.

17 See, e.g., the overlap between control and benefit enterprise liability outlined in Chapter 5.

18 Marco Cappelletti, *Justifying Strict Liability: A Comparative Analysis in Legal Reasoning* (OUP 2022).

19 Gray (n 5); Paula Giliker, 'Can the Supreme Court Halt the Ongoing Expansion of Vicarious Liability? *Barclays* and *Morrison* in the UK Supreme Court' (2021) 37 PN 55.

20 Craig Purshouse, 'Halting the Vicarious Liability Juggernaut: *Barclays Bank PLC v Various Claimants*' (2020) 28 Med L Rev 794; James Goudkamp and James Plunkett, 'Vicarious Liability in Australia: On the Move?' (2017) 17 OUCLJ 162; Paula Giliker, 'Analysing Institutional Liability for Child Sexual Abuse in England and Wales and Australia: Vicarious Liability, Non-Delegable Duties and Statutory Intervention' (2018) 77 CLJ 506.

21 *CCWS* (n 8), [19]. Even in 2016, Lord Reed in *Cox v Ministry of Justice* [2016] UKSC 10 observed that developments in this area of law had 'not yet come to a stop' (at [1]).

22 *Barclays* (n 6), [27] (Lady Hale).

23 *BXB* (n 10), [82]; *MXX v A Secondary School* [2022] EWHC 2207 (QB), [200] (HHJ Carmel Wall); *TVZ & others v Manchester City Football Club Ltd* [2022] EWHC 7 (QB), [321] (Johnson J); *Blackpool Football Club Ltd v DSN* [2021] EWCA Civ 1352, [100]–[4] (Stuart-Smith LJ); *JXJ v The Province of Great Britain of the Institute of Brothers of the Christian Schools* [2020] EWHC 1914 (QB), [144] (Chamberlain J).

24 See, e.g., Mark James, *Sports Law* (3rd edn, Palgrave 2017) 87–90; Simon Gardiner et al., *Sports Law* (4th edn, Routledge 2012) 505–6; Jack Anderson, *Modern Sports Law* (Hart 2010) 242–5.

25 See, e.g., Philip Hutchinson, 'Who Shoulders the Blame? An Analysis of Vicarious Liability in the Sports Industry' (LawInSport, 03 October 2016).

26 See, e.g., Mark James and David McArdle, 'Player Violence, or Violent Players? Vicarious Liability for Sports Participants' (2004) 12 Tort L Rev 131; Neville Cox, 'Civil Liability for Foul Play in Sport' (2003) 54 NILQ 351; Steven Rubin, 'The Vicarious Liability of Professional Sports Team for On-the-Field Assaults Committed by their Players' (1999) 1 Va J Sports & L 266; Neil Tucker, 'Assumption of Risk and Vicarious Liability in Personal Injury Actions Brought by Professional Athletes' (1980) 1980 Duke LJ 742.

27 See, e.g., Michael Beloff et al., *Sports Law* (2nd edn, Hart 2012) 157–8; Jack Harris, 'A Sporting Chance' (2012) 162 NLJ 1248; Neil Parpworth, 'Vicarious Liability on the Rugby Union Field' (2008) 172 Justice of the Peace 572; Julian Summerhayes, 'Injury Liability: Off-the-Ball Player Attacks: Club Liability' (2008) 6 WSLR.

28 Phillip Morgan, 'Vicarious Liability and the Beautiful Game – Liability for Professional and Amateur Footballers?' (2018) 38 LS 242.

29 Anderson (n 24) 22.

30 The role of distributive justice (and its distinction from corrective justice) in relation to sports law is briefly touched upon by Benjamin Andoh et al., 'Personal Injuries in Professional Football – Legal Aspects (UK)' (2010) 3/4 ISLR 60. However, the authors simply conclude that an analysis of distributive justice is 'not too apparent' in this area of law (at 62).

31 The close connection test was first utilised in the UK in *Lister* (n 12), [20].

32 Paula Giliker, 'Vicarious Liability in the Common Law World: An Introduction' in Paula Giliker (ed), *Vicarious Liability in the Common Law World* (Hart 2022) 7.

33 Christine Beuermann, 'Discerning the Form at the Second Stage of Vicarious Liability' (2022) 81 CLJ 495.

34 James Brown, 'The Vicarious Liability of Sports Governing Bodies and Competition Organisers' (2023) 43 LS 221.

35 James Brown, 'Vicarious Liability for On-Loan Sports Participants' (2022) 22 ISLR 40.

36 James Brown, 'Vicarious Liability in Amateur Sport: The Problem with Unincorporated Associations' (LawInSport, 29 June 2023).

37 *TVZ* (n 23); *DSN* (n 23). For commentary on the latter, see Christine Beuermann, 'Vicarious Liability for Football Scouts' (2022) 138 LQR 170.

38 Mark James, 'Sport, Safety and Participation – The Year in Review 2018/19' (LawInSport, 15 May 2019).

39 Rachel Vorspan, '"Rational Recreation" and the Law: The Transformation of Popular Urban Leisure in Victorian England' (2000) 45 McGill LJ 891, 907–8.

40 Simon Deakin and Zoe Adams, *Markesinis and Deakin's Tort Law* (8th edn, OUP 2019) 558. Cf *Lister* (n 12), [40] (Lord Clyde).

41 [2008] EWCA Civ 689.

2 Vicarious Liability for On-the-Field Acts

Personal Injuries

Introduction

When discussing the appropriate scope of vicarious liability in sport, it perhaps makes sense to begin with the most obvious (and arguably most likely) scenario in which such liability is likely to arise: for personal injuries suffered on the field of play. In applying the close connection test to this context, some sports law scholars have maintained that it is an inherently troublesome exercise to draw a line between those on-field acts that are, and are not, within the course of employment.[1] In contrast, other commentators have resorted to an overly simplistic and elementary distinction between negligent and intentional acts in applying the close connection test from *Lister v Hesley Hall Ltd*.[2] This chapter subjects this distinction to critical analysis and explains, with reference to *Gravil v Carroll and Redruth Rugby Football Club*,[3] how a more granulated and theoretically informed approach is necessary. In particular, it argues that intentional on-the-field acts can be just as closely connected to an athlete's employment as negligent on-the-field acts. With this in mind, the following sections explore the two main theoretical rationales that were employed by the Court of Appeal in *Gravil* in order to justify the imposition of vicarious liability in that case.

As such, I firstly examine how the theory of deterrence may help to eradicate foul play on the field, particularly by those athletes who possess a penchant for violent behaviour. Some scholars, however, question the desirability of the deterrence rationale, and they argue that direct liability in negligence provides a more suitable method of deterring violent on-field conduct. I suggest that this claim is ultimately unconvincing, and I highlight several reasons – ranging from evidentiary difficulties to the availability of insurance – as to why vicarious liability is a more appropriate action than a negligence claim. That said, however, I also contend that there may be a number of practical reasons that explain why deterrence alone cannot provide a satisfactory justification for, or indicator of, on-field vicarious liability. Accordingly, it needs to be buttressed by – and likely subsidiary to – another relevant rationale.

DOI: 10.4324/9781032665870-2

With this in mind, the chapter claims that enterprise liability ought to be the most dominant theory in this context, and it aims to show how an assessment of the inherent risks of a sport provides the best method of determining the close connection test for on-the-field acts. However, it is noteworthy that the judgment in *Gravil* failed to recognise that a risk-based approach to vicarious liability may clash with an assessment of a sport's playing culture at the standard of care stage. I refer to this as the 'double-edged sword' problem, and the analysis in this chapter offers some potential solutions to this tension: the abandonment of the playing culture enquiry altogether; a heavier reliance on the benefit formulation of enterprise liability; and drawing a distinction between consent and risk. After concluding that none of these choices provide a perfect solution, I offer a rather innovative method of avoiding this conflict. In short, I propose that we ought to adopt a normative approach to the inherent risks of a sport at the standard of care stage but an empirical assessment of the inherent risks when considering the vicarious liability of a club. Although this suggestion is not without its difficulties, the final part of this chapter will show that such a distinction can be justified once the policy bases of both a negligence and vicarious liability claim are fully understood.

The Negligence-Intentional Divide

Negligent On-the-Field Acts

In the vast majority of cases involving on-field tortious injury, sports claimants will pursue an action in negligence. The primary reason for pursuing a negligence claim is to ensure that the injured party retains access to the applicable insurance policies of the tortfeasor's employing club.[4] Barring the case of *Gravil* (which is considered in more detail below),[5] alternative causes of action under trespass to the person – which requires evidence of an intentional act[6] – are rarely initiated, largely because most insurance policies exclude cover for deliberately inflicted injury.[7]

With this rider in mind, it is clear that the bar for establishing negligence is a relatively high one. Following Donaldson MR's clarification in *Condon v Basi* as to the applicable standard of care in sport,[8] judges have generally been cognisant of sport's social utility and the fact that many games are often played at a very fast speed by participants who are acting in the heat of the moment.[9] In addition, and as was made clear by Tuckey LJ in *Caldwell v Maguire and Fitzgerald*, courts are required to take into account the prevailing circumstances of any sporting contest, including 'its object, the demands inevitably made upon its contestants, its inherent dangers (if any), its rules, conventions and customs, and the standards, skills and judgment reasonably to be expected of a contestant'.[10] In other words, courts take into account the fact that risk is an intrinsic aspect of many sports, and that it is often 'part of the fundamental attraction to that sport in the first place'.[11] This is reinforced by the sentiments of Dyson LJ in *Blake v Galloway* when he maintained that:

> the participants are taken impliedly to consent to those contacts which can reasonably be expected to occur in the course of the game, and to assume the risk of injury from such contacts... But they do not assume "the risk of a savage blow out of all proportion to the occasion".[12]

Whenever negligence is established, however, the vicarious liability of the tortfeasor's employer becomes an important feature of the litigation. One of the first known examples of a sports club being held vicariously liable for on-the-field conduct occurred in *McCord v Cornforth and Swansea City AFC*,[13] where the latter was held vicariously liable for a negligent career-ending challenge committed by their captain, John Cornforth. Since then, and following a line of cases including *Watson and Bradford AFC v Gray and Huddersfield Town AFC*[14] and *Thomas v Thornton and Bramley Rugby League Club*,[15] the vicarious liability of sports clubs for the negligent actions of their players has reached an almost 'presumptive, uncontested status',[16] with the result that many later cases have not even listed the tortfeasing athlete as a defendant in the proceedings.[17]

This is unsurprising in light of Lord Phillips' comments in *Various Claimants v Catholic Child Welfare Society* which suggest that, '[w]here the tortfeasor does something that he is required or requested to do pursuant to his relationship with the defendant in a manner that is negligent, [the course of employment] test is likely to be satisfied'.[18] Indeed, it is perhaps of little surprise that, since the seminal case of *Lister*, the majority of cases dealing with the course of employment criterion have related to *intentional* acts perpetrated by the tortfeasor. As such, and to translate this to the sporting context, vicarious liability for on-field negligence is simply now par for course because of its 'integral connection with the player's employment by the club'.[19]

Intentional On-the-Field Acts

In contrast to negligent acts, it is perhaps less clear-cut whether vicarious liability will arise for deliberately violent on-the-field acts. Seemingly in line with the comments made by Cox,[20] Beloff et al. maintain that a club is unlikely to be held responsible for an employee's deliberate act, and that only negligent or reckless injury will trigger vicarious liability.[21] However, whilst it might be acceptable to argue normatively that this ought to be the case, it is far more problematic, from a descriptive point of view, to suggest that this *is* the case. After all, one can identify numerous examples in recent years of various intentional acts – such as a racist attack at a petrol station,[22] an assault at an after-work Christmas party[23] and the sexual abuse of a child by a foster parent[24] – that were deemed to be within the course of employment.

The apparent problem with Beloff et al.'s conclusion here, then, is that their analysis relies primarily on pre-*Lister* case law.[25] Throughout the twentieth century, the outcome of cases was largely predicated on the second limb of the so-called Salmond test, which asked whether a particular tortious act was a 'wrongful and unauthorised mode of doing some act authorised by the master'.[26] This gave rise to the presumption that intentional harm would rarely (if ever) lead to vicarious liability,[27] as Stevens correctly suggested that it would be stretching language beyond credulity to argue that many deliberate acts (such as sexual abuse) could be described in any way as an improper mode of doing an authorised act.[28] Perhaps in light of the intuition that the claimant in *Lister* was a deserving victim, various judges in this case – most notably Lords Steyn and Millett – laid the Salmond test to rest and introduced a broader test of 'close connection'.[29] It was much easier to find vicarious liability for intentional acts on the basis of this test, for it was far more logical to say, for instance, that sexual abuse was closely connected to a particular individual's employment.

The incorrectness of Beloff et al.'s analysis is also neatly illustrated by the outcome in *Gravil*. In this case, the claimant, Andrew Gravil, was playing for Halifax Rugby Football Club when he was punched in the face by an opposition player following a post-scrum melee in a rugby union game. The blow, which occurred after the referee's whistle had gone, caused a blow-out fracture of Gravil's right orbit. After successfully demonstrating an actionable battery against the initial tortfeasor, Richard Carroll, the claimant also sought to establish the vicarious liability of Carroll's employer at the time, Redruth Rugby Football Club. In overruling the findings of Gray J in the Bristol District Registry, the Court of Appeal agreed with the claimant's contention that Redruth ought to be held responsible for this harm. Clarke MR suggested that it was 'fair and just to hold the club vicariously responsible for the injury to the claimant',[30] and he attempted to buttress this reasoning with reference to two particular theories.

The first was that of deterrence. In particular, the Court of Appeal's view in *Gravil* was that the imposition of vicarious liability would encourage many sports clubs to adequately discipline any athlete who flagrantly breaches the rules of the game.[31] The second reason for holding Redruth responsible for this harm was centred around the fact that off-the-ball melees occurred with such frequency in rugby that they could reasonably be regarded as 'part of the game'.[32] Clarke MR was thus eager to stress that the throwing of punches was an 'ordinary (though undesirable) incident of a rugby match', and it was something that 'both clubs would have expected to occur'.[33] Although His Honour did not explicitly use the term, this was (in all but name) an argument based on enterprise liability. Indeed, and as Chamallas notes, an examination of the foreseeability and frequency of a particular act forms the basis of an enterprise risk enquiry,[34] and it is perhaps for such reasons that other scholars have suggested that risk could be closely aligned with the notion of causation.[35]

With this in mind, a number of observations can be made about this case. First, it is relevant that *Gravil* remains the only UK case to consider the vicarious liability of a sports club for deliberate on-the-field conduct.[36] This paucity of cases is perhaps best explained by the evidential difficulties in proving intention in a fast-paced physically invasive sport, as well as by the so-called sporting omerta (which suggests that many sporting communities subscribe to the adage that 'what happens on the pitch, stays on the pitch').[37] As such, it is likely that an assessment of the close connection test in relation to on-the-field injuries will only be necessary for those scenarios that involve some particularly egregious off-the-ball act.

Second, *Gravil* confirms that there is now little need to resort to this unhelpful negligence-intentional divide in establishing the closeness of connection in each scenario. It may often be the case that some intentional acts are just as intrinsic to a particular sport as a negligent or mistimed challenge. Take, for instance, the 'beanball' pitch in professional baseball, a practice which involves the pitcher intentionally throwing the ball at a batter's head. Roser-Jones observes that this is now 'an accepted custom in baseball, where pitchers known for their hits are commonly referred to as "headhunters", and managers order such hits strategically'.[38]

Finally, and on a point of broader significance, it is clear from the surrounding literature on *Gravil* that remarkably little attention has been paid to the application of the close connection test in this case. Despite judicial comments suggesting that the fundamental issue in this litigation was the potential liability of clubs for off-the-ball assaults,[39] the vast majority of scholarly analysis following this case has focussed on the potential employment status of semi-professional athletes,[40] with many commentators seemingly content to assume that punching an opposition player is in fact an inherent aspect of contemporary rugby. The following analysis seeks to fill in this lacuna by offering a detailed analysis of the two dominant theories that were utilised in order to justify the satisfaction of the close connection test in *Gravil*: deterrence and enterprise risk. It will be argued that, whilst the concept of deterrence could be a useful theoretical consideration in the context of on-the-field acts, it cannot, by itself, provide a satisfactory indicator of vicarious liability. Not only does this help to reinforce the commitment to theory that underpins my approach to vicarious liability, but it also paves the way for viewing enterprise liability as the stronger theoretical consideration in this context.

Vicarious Liability and the Deterrence of Violent Play

As outlined by Fleming, the basic premise of the deterrence rationale is that, by holding the employer vicariously liable, 'the law furnishes an incentive to discipline servants guilty of wrongdoing'.[41] This logic was explicitly utilised by Clarke MR in *Gravil* when he held that:

> [t]he line between playing hard and playing dirty may be seen as a fine one. The temptation for players to cross the line in the scrum may be considerable unless active steps are taken by clubs to deter them from doing so... It is perhaps striking that here the club did not take any disciplinary action against the first defendant. Perhaps it would have done if it had appreciated that there was a risk of liability in such cases in the future.[42]

It is notable that various sports law scholars who have touched upon the issue of vicarious liability in sport have been persuaded by such reasoning. As Anderson writes, 'on pain of vicarious liability, clubs will be motivated to materially decrease the risk of their employee-players misbehaving on the field of play'.[43] Other commentators appear to refer to deterrence-based reasoning when discussing vicarious liability for athletes who demonstrate a 'propensity for violence on the pitch'.[44] In sporting jargon, such athletes are often endearingly referred to by fans and pundits as 'hard men' or 'enforcers'.[45] In this light, James and McArdle explain that:

> [w]here the club knows of a player's propensity to violent or aggressive play, and either buys him for that reason or continues to pick him despite his playing in that manner, then vicarious liability should attach.[46]

Morgan appears to make a similar point when he opines that clubs ought to think twice about selecting players who have a penchant for violence.[47] In his view, if a club 'encourages aggressive behaviour in a player outside of the rules of the game, for instance by instructing them to act as an on-pitch "enforcer"... vicarious liability for their on-pitch acts of violence is likely'.[48] This line of reasoning is perhaps best illustrated by the US case of *Tomjanovich v California Sports Inc*.[49] Here, the claimant (a professional basketball player in the National Basketball Association) was seriously injured after being punched in the face by Kermit Washington, an opposition player representing the Los Angeles Lakers. Washington had been hired by the club primarily to act as an 'enforcer' on the court, and the Lakers were clearly well aware of – and perhaps even impressed by – the tortfeasor's propensity for violence. This was illustrated by the fact that the club had persuaded Washington to 'appear in a Sports Illustrated article on basketball's "enforcers"'.[50] As such, the Supreme Court of California had no hesitation in holding the Lakers vicariously liable for the harm suffered by Tomjanovich.[51]

Now, one might assume from these judicial and scholarly comments that deterrence is a paramount consideration when determining the appropriate scope of vicarious liability for on-the-field acts. There are, however, two arguments that may significantly limit the desirability of the deterrence rationale in this context. Let us call these the *suitability argument* and the *practicality argument*. The purpose of the following two sections is to highlight that, whilst the *suitability argument* provides an unconvincing reason for rejecting the theory of deterrence, the *practicality argument* demonstrates the need for deterrence to be buttressed by (and subsidiary to) another relevant rationale: that of enterprise liability.

Direct Liability: A More Suitable Cause of Action?

The crux of the *suitability argument* is that the deterrence of violent on-the-field conduct is better dealt with by primary liability in negligence. For instance, McBride and Bagshaw suggest that the reasoning adopted in *Gravil* is somewhat curious given that even prudent disciplinary action by the rugby club would not have barred the operation of vicarious liability.[52] As other scholars have explained, strict liability is unconcerned with the steps taken by a defendant to prevent harm, so it might be said that vicarious liability provides no incentive for employers to deter injury-causing behaviour.[53] In their view, fault-based liability is better suited to the achievement of deterrence, because an employer under this form of liability can avoid a damages award if they can show that they took all reasonable care. This was the argument outlined by McPeak when she observed that 'deterrence goals are not furthered when the actor's conduct results in liability regardless of the level of care used'.[54]

Such arguments could perhaps be further reinforced by the Court of Appeal's judgment in *Mattis v Pollock*.[55] This case concerned a nightclub bouncer (Mr Cranston) exacting revenge on a patron by stabbing him in the back. Much like the Lakers in the *Tomjanovich* litigation, the employer here was clearly aware of Cranston's violent nature, and it was this reputation that led to his employment. The nightclub owner had specifically intended to employ a 'bully' in order to both respond to a 'weak door' and to 'intimidate customers'.[56] Whilst Judge LJ found that vicarious liability was established on these facts, he did conclude that, had it been necessary to decide the issue, he would have held the employer personally liable under negligence for knowingly employing a bouncer with 'aggressive tendencies, which he encouraged rather than curbed'.[57] Giliker argues that it would have been far more appropriate to impose direct liability on the nightclub owner here,[58] and other academic and judicial commentators appear to agree with this stance.[59] Binnie J in *Jacobi v Griffiths*, for example, commented that 'an undue emphasis on the deterrence factor may blur the line between vicarious liability and negligence', and he stressed that we ought to consider 'developing and refining the paths of potential direct liability' for many employment-related harms.[60]

Now, whilst this line of reasoning may at first glance be intuitive, I must express my disagreement with the *suitability argument* here. In particular, this argument overlooks the fact that there may be serious evidentiary difficulties in proving that a club knowingly hired a so-called 'hard man'. It is highly questionable whether a judge (or indeed any other individual) is able to determine, with sufficient clarity, whether a particular athlete possesses a penchant for violence. Certainly, assessing the number of fouls committed and/or cards received by a player will not do, particularly as bookings can be received for a host of reasons besides violent play (e.g. time-wasting or handball).

The reality is that it will be very difficult to establish that a club knowingly employed an on-field enforcer, and it is for such reasons that vicarious liability is the preferred cause of action for injuries suffered on the field of play. Unlike a claim in negligence, vicarious liability does not necessarily require proof that the club was aware of an athlete's volatile tendencies, and this will allow them to internalise the costs of selecting (and perhaps even encouraging the behaviour of) supposedly violent players.[61] In this regard, by motivating clubs to identify more effective ways of reducing their accident costs, Sharkey is correct to argue that 'strict-vicarious liability has an edge over direct employer negligence liability in terms of optimal deterrence'.[62]

This is not, however, the only reason for rejecting the *suitability argument*. In fact, there may be an additional justification rooted in the theory of loss spreading that helps to further explain why vicarious liability is a more appropriate tool for deterring on-the-field violence. In sum, whilst direct intentional acts of the employer are typically not covered by an insurance policy,[63] an employer held *vicariously* liable for an intentional act will be able to rely on their insurers to foot the bill.[64] This was made clear in the case of *Hawley v Luminar Leisure Ltd*, where it was held that the employer of a bouncer who had intentionally inflicted grievous bodily harm on the victim could in fact recover from their accident-only liability policy, because the employer had not themselves been guilty of a deliberate act.[65] Consequently, it is likely that both the injured claimant and the defendant club would agree that a vicarious liability claim is more desirable than a negligence claim in this context.

The Practicality of Deterrence

Whilst I have argued above that the *suitability argument* does not provide a compelling critique of the deterrence rationale in relation to on-the-field acts, the *practicality argument* perhaps provides a more convincing reason for doubting the utility of deterrence in this context. In essence, the *practicality argument* encapsulates two concerns. The first is that it would be impractical (and perhaps undesirable) to rely on the theory of deterrence in the absence of empirical evidence. Without further empirical data to support any claim, we should be wary of relying too heavily on deterrence. For instance, I could quite easily refute Clarke MR's claim in *Gravil* by simply stating that the imposition of vicarious liability would *not* encourage clubs to take further disciplinary action against its players. But of course, in the absence of further evidence, this is just one speculative claim against another, and it is likely to only produce moot arguments and 'bald assertions'.[66] As such, we ought to remember Atiyah's timely warning that 'the case for imposing vicarious liability on the ground that it forwards the policy of accident prevention must… be regarded as largely not proven'.[67]

The second reason for doubting the deterrence rationale relates to its seemingly illimitable boundaries. In particular, deterrence does not seem to provide a satisfactory method for determining what particular acts a sports club will be held vicariously liable for. In fact, deterrence would presumably lead to vicarious liability for *every* on-field act, because we should want to deter all negligent and intentional harm (no matter how far removed from the game it is). Deterrence may provide a convincing justification for the existence of vicarious liability, but it provides a rather impractical framework for determining whether the doctrine should be imposed or not.

As such, I must express my agreement with Kirby J in the Australian case of *New South Wales v Lepore*. There, he recognised that deterrence was 'neither the main nor only factor to consider in judging whether vicarious liability is imposed by the law'.[68] As highlighted above, deterrence certainly has a role to play in determining the appropriate scope of vicarious liability in sport. However, in light of the practical limitations of deterrence that have been considered here, it needs to be supported by (or subsidiary to) another relevant rationale.[69] As the following section illustrates, enterprise liability may be able to respond to these deficiencies in the theory of deterrence.

Vicarious Liability, Enterprise Liability and the Problem with 'Playing Culture'

The discussion so far has suggested that, whilst vicarious liability provides a more suitable method of deterring violent on-field conduct than direct liability, there are several practical issues associated with the theory of deterrence. As such, it is maintained that deterrence ought to play a secondary role to the more prominent theory of enterprise liability when determining the appropriate scope of vicarious liability for on-the-field acts. This position is broadly consistent with the Canadian perspective on vicarious liability. As Neyers and Kiss have recently illustrated, the combined deterrence and enterprise liability justification from *Bazley v Curry* 'forms the bedrock' of the Canadian courts' justification of the doctrine, but it is 'enterprise risk [that] has taken on the most significance' in many judgments.[70]

This interplay between enterprise liability and deterrence was seemingly overlooked, however, by Clarke MR in *Gravil*, as he made no attempt to establish which theory ought to be the most dominant in this context. As I have argued elsewhere, if we wish to provide a more meaningful and transparent law on vicarious liability, then it is worth examining more explicitly how the relative weight of these rationales may differ depending on the context in question.[71] Consequently, whilst the judgment in *Gravil* is to be commended for its theoretical analysis of vicarious liability, it could have been improved further had Clarke MR expanded on the weight to be afforded to both deterrence and enterprise liability in the context of on-the-field personal injuries.[72]

It is also worth remembering here that Clarke MR focussed predominantly on the risk-related formulation of enterprise liability in his judgment. Now, it is easy to see why he did so. After all, and as Nixon outlines, many sports could perhaps best be described as giving rise to a 'culture of risk' in which injuries and harmful activities are normalised.[73] Given that participation in some sports thus requires participants to subject themselves to a 'higher-than-normal level of risk',[74] it may seem appropriate to assess the inherency of these risks in relation to each particular sport to assess whether vicarious liability ought to be imposed.[75] This coincides with the general judicial consensus that the concept of enterprise liability will be the 'most influential' determinant of an employer's vicarious responsibility.[76]

Additionally, focussing on what risks are inherent to, and expected to occur in, each sport provides us with the adaptability to consider the changing norms and informal rules of that particular game. For instance, with the aid of rule changes by the International Rugby Board, it is clear to see how acceptable conduct in rugby union scrums has evolved over the years.[77] Likewise, and to take a further example, a football player's approach to aerial duels has arguably changed over time. According to one FIFA spokesman, players in the modern game are more frequently raising their elbows during aerial challenges,[78] with the result that any injury caused by a flailing elbow is perhaps now more likely to be regarded as an ordinary and expected incident of contemporary football. As such, given that the informal culture of a particular sport is 'evidently quite elastic',[79] a flexible risk-based approach may provide the most satisfactory indicator of vicarious liability in this context. Furthermore, and in contrast to deterrence, we might also say that risk provides the most meaningful justification for liability here, as it furnishes us not only with the reason for *why* an employer is held responsible but also a more focussed method for determining *what* acts the employer ought to be held liable for.

However, whilst I find the notion of risk a convincing rationale for imposing liability in this context, it must be noted that the determination of vicarious liability based on the ordinary and inherent risks of a sport is open to criticism. The primary difficulty here, which was not identified in *Gravil*, lies in the fact that a risk-based approach to vicarious liability seems to clash with the assessment of a sport's playing culture that is used to determine whether a tortious act was committed by an athlete in the first place. To be clear, a sport's playing culture is considered as part of an action in both negligence and trespass. For negligence claims, it is considered at the standard of care stage; in trespass cases, it is considered as part of the defence of consent.[80] For purposes of consistency, and because negligence is usually the preferred cause of action for injured sports claimants, the following analysis will primarily refer to the notion of playing culture at the standard of care stage.

Now, in order to illustrate the potential clash between vicarious liability and the requirements of the underlying tort in this context, it is worth briefly explaining what is meant by reference to a sport's playing culture here. According to Murphy, Williams and Dunning, sport, like many other social activities, 'can be conducted in terms of a "spirit" or ethos which condones rule infractions to a greater or lesser degree'.[81] This quote nicely captures the essence of a sport's playing culture, a concept that has otherwise been understood to mean a 'normative system inside of and parallel to the formal regulatory framework of the sport'.[82] In sum, then, it suggests that those acts that occur with such frequency and impunity in a particular sport are understood and consented to by all participants, despite the fact that the specific act in question might be contrary to the official rules of the game.[83]

By way of example, James and McArdle argue that the incident in *Caldwell* – which involved a professional jockey suffering serious injuries after the 'careless riding' of the two defendants – was one that 'occurred very frequently within national hunt racing, [so] it could be seen as an integral part of the sport's playing culture'.[84] As the trial judge in *Caldwell* explained, whilst the harm in this case was, in theory, avoidable, it was something that was 'bound to occur from time to time'.[85] Judges will, therefore, take into account a number of factors – such as the nature of the sport, the level at which it is played, and the type of act committed (as well as the frequency with which it occurs) – in order to determine whether certain conduct is within a sport's playing culture.[86] If it is, then the harm will be considered to be an acceptable and inherent risk of that sport, and the injurer will not be held to have breached their duty of care.

This, however, is where a risk-based approach to vicarious liability may run into trouble. In short, considering a sport's playing culture at the standard of care stage may lead to what Tucker has identified as a 'classic catch-22' scenario here. In his words, '[i]f the possibility that the reckless misconduct of an employee will injure an opponent is an "inevitable toll" of business, it is incongruous to say at the same time that the athlete does not assume the risk of injury'.[87] As such, the 'type of action that could result in employer liability should, at the same time, bar the plaintiff's action altogether, because it must have been foreseen'.[88]

To be sure, let us consider again the facts of *Gravil*. If punching truly is an 'ordinary' and 'expected' element of modern rugby (as the Court of Appeal proposed), does this not suggest that Gravil's battery claim should have been automatically struck out on the grounds that he implicitly consented to this harm as part of rugby union's playing culture?[89] On the flip side, if the blow to Gravil was not part of the intrinsic risks as defined by rugby's playing culture – and thus a form of negligence or an actionable trespass – then the argument for finding a close connection between Carroll's punch and his employment is, on the basis of enterprise liability at least, greatly weakened.

There is certainly a double-edged sword here, in that the more acts that we think are inherent to the playing of a particular sport for the purposes of vicarious liability, the more we potentially remove from the scope of negligence (and trespass) to negate a breach of duty in the first place. Unfortunately, with the exception of Tucker's analysis, the few works that have touched upon the issue of vicarious liability in the sporting context have yet to recognise this tension. James and McArdle, for instance, suggest that a 'poorly executed' tackle would give rise to a 'relatively straightforward case of vicarious liability', because challenges 'made with more force than is necessary are an integral part of the playing of most contact sports and are consented to by the players'.[90] However, if a tackle was implicitly consented to by a player, then surely no negligence or trespass could be established in the first place, meaning that there is no wrongful act upon which to base the vicarious liability of an employer. The quandary was seemingly so perplexing to Tucker that he concluded that we should hold only 'the participant-defendant, but not the team, liable' in every case.[91] This is, of course, a rather unacceptable response insofar as it provides a *de jure* immunity to sports clubs for any harmful conduct that occurs on the field of play.

As such, the following sections aim to explore some potential solutions to this so-called 'catch-22'. In particular, I assess the following four suggestions: the desirability of ignoring the playing culture of a sport at the standard of care stage altogether; the prospect of relying more heavily on the benefit formulation of enterprise liability to supplement (or even replace) a risk-based approach to on-the-field acts; the feasibility of distinguishing the inherent risks of a sport from the implied consent of sporting participants; and the possibility of adopting an empirical conception of the inherent customs of a sport for vicarious liability purposes but a normative approach when assessing the inherent risks of a sport for the purposes of the initial negligence/trespass claim. It will be concluded that the final suggestion offers the most desirable solution to the double-edged sword problem.

Abandoning Playing Culture

The first – and perhaps the simplest – option to avoid the double-edged sword problem is to do away with an assessment of a sport's playing culture altogether. If we do not examine the inherent risks of a sport at the standard of care stage, there will, of course, be nothing to clash with when adopting an enterprise risk-based approach to a vicarious liability claim. Interestingly, some scholars have already advocated for the elimination of the playing culture enquiry. For instance, both Grayson and Voicu believe that liability for on-field conduct ought to be regulated solely by reference to the official guidelines and rulebooks of each sport.[92] For them, any foul, no matter how minor, should be actionable.

However, from a normative perspective, the abandonment of the playing culture consideration is likely to lead to undesirable results in practice. If all minor fouls (such as a slight push in football or basketball) could give rise to liability, it is likely that many sports would be swamped with negligence claims. One of the main advantages of considering a sport's playing culture is that it removes injuries from low-level fouls from the purview of negligence. If we accept that sport is designed to be played on the pitch and not in courtrooms across the UK – and that legal action should be reserved only for the most egregious on-field behaviour – then an analysis of a sport's playing culture is crucial. Indeed, and as Fogel writes, it is 'not in the public interest or good for the courts to be filled with cases of on-field violence, as this would burden the courts and undermine the integrity and sustainability of many sports'.[93] In this light, it might be said that an assessment of a sport's playing culture serves an important instrumentalist purpose: that is, it operates as a tool to fulfil the wider policy goal of facilitating participation in sport.

Aside from this normative argument, it also seems unlikely, from a predictive point of view, that courts will turn a blind eye to a sport's playing culture at the standard of care stage. Recent case law appears to confirm that many judges are in favour of considering a sport's playing culture, and that a breach of a sporting rule ought not to automatically lead to a finding of liability.[94] This is neatly encapsulated in Lord Jones' judgment in *McMahon v Dear*, a case which concerned a personal injury action against a golfer who blinded the claimant in one eye. After referring to The R&A's 'Rules of Golf' in this case, his Lordship admitted that:

> in searching for the meaning of the safety guidelines, I am not performing the same task as I would be if construing a statute or interpreting a contract. What I need to do is determine, as a matter of fact *and in practical terms*, what the golfer ought to do during the round, if following the guidance.[95]

A Greater Role for Benefit Enterprise Liability

The second option to respond to the catch-22 identified in *Gravil* is to rely more heavily on the benefit formulation of enterprise liability (as opposed to its risk-based formulation). Indeed, there is arguably more scope for an assessment of benefit enterprise liability in the on-the-field context than some judges may care to admit. Whilst Clarke MR briefly mentioned that 'undetected foul play may be perceived to advance the club's interests',[96] Gray J in an earlier appeal maintained that it was somewhat of a stretch to classify Carroll's on-field brawl as benefitting his club in any way. In his view, the conduct was more likely to harm Redruth because the player had been sent to the sin bin, and he was subsequently banned from the sport for eight weeks.[97]

However, just because a club was negatively impacted in one respect (losing a player) does not necessarily mean that they do not benefit in other ways. For instance, it may have been that Carroll's aggressive conduct during the game intimidated the opposition and put them off their game. Likewise, had it been established that Gravil was a star player for his team, it is easy to see how Redruth would have benefitted from taking him out of the game before he could inflict any serious sportive damage. Additionally, a club may also benefit from one of their players engaging in underhanded behaviour that is designed to rile up the opposition. If it could be shown that the brawl in *Gravil* only occurred because Carroll was hoping to provoke a reaction from the opposition that would be detected by the referee,[98] then a fairness-based rationale could equally justify imposing vicarious liability on Redruth here.

Finally, and more broadly, there may also be longer-term financial benefits from an employee engaging in violent on-field behaviour. One might consider here the common practice of fighting in ice hockey. Rubin notes that club owners are generally supportive of fighting on the rink, as they view such conduct as a 'necessary marketing tool' that helps to sell tickets.[99] In this light, there are ample ways in which the benefit formulation of enterprise liability might be able to justify vicarious liability for on-the-field acts. If this is so, one ought to keep in mind three wider points about the role of benefit enterprise liability in this context.

First, this application of vicarious liability to sport neatly illustrates that an employer may still benefit from an activity even if they concomitantly suffer some form of loss from it. This appears to fit nicely alongside Lord Reed's more liberal interpretation of 'benefit' in *Cox v Ministry of Justice*, where he highlighted that the benefit an employer derives from the tortfeasor's activities need not be profit-making.[100]

Second, the benefit formulation of enterprise liability may tentatively suggest that vicarious liability for on-the-field acts is more likely to occur in professional sport. This is due to the partisan nature of professional sport, and the fact that elite clubs are more likely to accrue a significant financial and/or sporting benefit from the success that may be attributed to violent on-field behaviour.

Third, it may be that the justification for vicarious liability is seemingly at its strongest whenever benefit overlaps with the risk-related formulation of enterprise liability. To take one example, this would mean that there is a very strong case for imposing vicarious liability on an ice hockey team if one of their employees intentionally injures an opposition player during an on-rink fight. Fighting is an inherent risk of ice hockey, and the employer appears to be gaining a benefit from this conduct. In line with the discussion in the previous section, this conclusion may be further strengthened if the tortfeasor was considered an on-field enforcer by his employer.

Of course, however, it is unlikely that the benefit formulation of enterprise liability could be exclusively relied upon to establish vicarious liability. As the above application to *Gravil* highlights, almost all on-field acts – no matter how egregious or unrelated to a sport – could be seen as conferring at least some form of loose benefit on an employer, and this may lead to an almost illimitable scope of vicarious liability. Indeed, Priest appears to raise similar concerns in his seminal work on enterprise liability.[101] As such, whilst benefit enterprise liability could certainly occupy a more relevant status than that envisaged by Gray J in *Gravil*, it could only really supplement – rather than completely replace – a risk-based approach (which, if analysed with reference to relevant empirical data as suggested later in this chapter, arguably has more defined limits than the benefit formulation). As such, if risk is still being used as a criterion to determine vicarious liability in this context, then the double-edged sword problem is still a live issue.

Distinguishing Consent and Risk

A third potential solution to the catch-22 problem might be to distinguish the implied consent of sporting participants from their knowledge of the inherent risks of the sport. Although we have seen the conflation of these two concepts in Dyson LJ's judgment in *Blake*,[102] it may be possible to differentiate them here. We might say, in line with the views of some scholars, that playing culture is concerned with the issue of implied consent.[103] In contrast, vicarious liability is perhaps more appropriately concerned with the (wider) notion of what risks are inherent to a particular sport. It may not necessarily be the case that an individual can be said to impliedly consent to (or accept) every reasonably foreseeable risk.

This is evident in Beever's work when he highlights that, whilst most car owners will be aware of the inherent risks of getting behind the wheel, this does not automatically mean that they consent to the risk of being injured by another individual's dangerous driving. If this were the case, he explains, 'then only the insane or ignorant could sue for road accidents'.[104] Lord Denning in *Nettleship v Weston* also made a similar point when he suggested that '[k]nowledge of the risk of injury is not enough' to constitute a successful defence of *volenti*.[105] Consequently, whilst the risk of a road accident is one that most reasonable drivers are aware of, it is not a risk that they are necessarily willing to accept for the purposes of implied consent.

Can this reasoning be equally transposed to the sporting context, and in particular, to the facts of *Gravil*? Not quite. According to Pendlebury's empirical study into the perception of playing culture amongst rugby union athletes, many participants are not only aware of the potential risk of being punched, but many in fact also *consent* to it as part of the sport. In the author's words, 'punching is seemingly accepted by the rugby union participants as an integral part of the game'.[106] To the extent that most players *accept* the risk of a punch (rather than just merely being aware of the risk), the double-edged sword problem from *Gravil* is still an active concern. This is seemingly confirmed by the recent analysis of Deakin and Adams who suggest that:

> ...if a foul is committed in the course of a game, consent can normally be assumed for the purposes of both a battery and a negligence claim, unless the conduct of the defendant is completely beyond normal expectations of the participants in some way.[107]

Interestingly, punching is not the only act that appears to be within the 'normal expectations' of rugby union players. In fact, the overwhelming majority of respondents to Pendlebury's empirical study also suggested that kicking another player on the field was an act that was implicitly consented to by participants.[108] The line was drawn, however, in regard to an off-the-ball headbutt. Most players were of the view that such conduct 'could not, and should never, be accepted as part of the game'.[109] The respondents appeared to justify this conclusion by reference to the fact that they had never seen a headbutt occur on the field of play before.[110] Two brief concluding points ought to be made here. First, it may be tentatively suggested that, had Carroll headbutted (rather than punched) Gravil during the post-scrum melee, Clarke MR ought not to have found vicarious liability in this case quite so readily. Second, and on a related point, such empirical data illustrates that risk may do a better job of reining in overly broad liability than benefit enterprise liability.

A Normative-Empirical Dichotomy

Although distinguishing between consent and risk does not seem to provide a satisfactory answer to the double-edged sword problem, drawing a distinction between a normative and empirical enquiry may provide a more effective solution. In order to illustrate how this normative-empirical dichotomy might work in practice, we firstly need to unpack how judges determine the playing culture of a sport. According to Lord Woolf CJ in *R v Barnes*, an assessment of a sport's playing culture is a necessarily 'objective one' that 'does not depend upon the views of individual players'.[111] In other words, judges are currently required to conduct a normative analysis of the standard of care in each case to determine which on-field acts *they* think are deserving of civil (or criminal) liability.

This point is made clear in *R v Billinghurst*,[112] a criminal case in which the defendant rugby player, not unlike the incident in *Gravil*, punched an opposing scrum-half in the face during an off-the-ball incident. Despite hearing testimonial evidence from other professional rugby players to the tune that punching in rugby was 'the rule rather than the exception',[113] Billinghurst was found guilty and sentenced to nine months' imprisonment (suspended for two years). Pendlebury insightfully argues that the court in *Billinghurst* were 'determined to point out that even if punching is part of the actual playing culture of rugby, it is not part of the playing culture as defined by the court'.[114]

This gives rise to a crucial (and somewhat novel) distinction, particularly when we recall my preference for a model of vicarious liability that draws on empirical evidence. Given that an empirical approach will generally legiti-mise a much wider range of acts than a normative judicial decision, it might be that the catch-22 identified in *Gravil* could be rationalised by separating the empirical and normative dimensions of the enquiry. In this regard, and from a normative judicial standpoint, an off-the-ball punch would not be within the *court's* conception of rugby union's playing culture. On this basis, anyone who commits such an act will be held to have breached their duty of care towards the injured party. In contrast, however, when we come to empirically assess the vicarious liability of the wrongdoer's club for this harm, Pendle-bury's study would suggest that such a punch was an inherent and expected risk of rugby union. When viewed in this light, an empirical conception of vicarious liability may provide a solution to the double-edged sword problem that has long bemused scholars such as Tucker.

As a result, claimants who wish to establish the vicarious liability of a sports club for an intentional on-the-field act ought to strongly consider pre-senting some form of empirical evidence to support their proposition that the wrongdoer's conduct was an ordinary and foreseeable risk of a certain sport. In light of the current sparsity of qualitative projects that touch upon this is-sue,[115] this will likely require counsel for the claimant to conduct their own investigation into the frequency of such an act, similar to that found in both *Billinghurst* and *Blissett*.

To clarify how such an approach might work in practice, let us examine another scenario in which vicarious liability might be imposed upon a sports club. Consider, for instance, the creation of 'hit lists' or 'bounties', whereby players (and oftentimes coaches) pool together money in order to pay out bonuses to those who injure opposition players. Such a practice has been al-leged to occur in both rugby league[116] and ice hockey,[117] although it is widely considered to be most prominent in American football. This is evidenced by the New Orleans Saints 2009 bounty scandal, in which the club's defensive co-ordinator, Gregg Williams, administered additional bounty payments to those Saints players who deliberately injured the opposition. These payments were doubled (or sometimes even tripled) when the club entered the play-offs, with players receiving the most money for a 'knock-out' hit.[118]

Of course, when a coach participates in (and even administers) the bounty, it will be a relatively simple matter of holding the club vicariously liable for the negligent actions of the coach.[119] Nevertheless, let us assume here that only one or two players were involved in the creation and execution of a hit-list,[120] and the club is unaware of this practice. In this instance, the courts are never likely to regard the creation of a hit-list as being within the playing culture of American football – and rightly so, given that it would impede an otherwise meritorious claim against the wrongdoer in negligence or trespass.

However, many former and current NFL players have admitted that the creation of hit lists is a rather common practice in American football, and something that is generally accepted as an ordinary aspect of the sport.[121] According to the former defensive back Matt Bowen, the placing of bounties on opposition players is a 'fundamental part of the NFL's culture that isn't talked about outside of team facilities'.[122] He outlined that, during his time at the Washington Commanders (formerly Washington Redskins), the construction of hit lists was a 'common practice' for the team, with money being awarded for 'big hits' that took an opposing player 'out of the game'.[123] On this basis, we can see that an empirical assessment of such practices would likely point towards the vicarious liability of the tortfeasor's club, despite the fact that the placing of bounties would never be considered by a court to be normatively within the playing culture of American football. This conclusion would be further reinforced by the fact that the employing club were receiving an apparent benefit from the actions of their employees.

Potential Objections to a Normative-Empirical Dichotomy

Now, there may be some difficulties associated with this normative-empirical dichotomy. However, unlike with the other alternatives highlighted above, none of the difficulties mentioned here ought necessarily to be seen as fatal to this suggestion.

The first objection is a rather simple one: many may question whether it is incongruous to adopt a normative approach to the inherent risks of a sport for the purposes of breach of duty but then to adopt an empirical test when we come to assess the vicarious liability of the club. Might this lead to unnecessary confusion and inconsistency in this area of law? Perhaps. My feeling, however, is that this normative-empirical dichotomy could be justified by highlighting the different policy bases underlying both negligence and vicarious liability. In regards to an assessment of the inherent risks for the underlying tort, various scholars have correctly highlighted that deference to the views of individual athletes is likely to 'excuse overly violent (and often cowardly and cynical) play',[124] with the result that it grants athletes an unparalleled 'license for thuggery'.[125] Consequently, in order to ensure that an appreciation of a sport's playing culture does not lead to the unreasonable maintenance of the (oftentimes anti-progressive) status quo, judges have adopted a normative stance to the level of acceptable violence in each sport.

This policy concern is clearly not applicable, though, when dealing with vicarious liability. In fact, an empirical assessment of the inherent sporting risks for the purposes of vicarious liability is likely to *widen* – rather than restrict – the potential for compensation, because an athlete's perception of acceptable risk is likely to legitimise a broader array of on-the-field acts. Consequently, rather than being seen as upholding an anti-progressive stance, adopting an empirical approach for vicarious liability purposes could instead be celebrated for providing a more pragmatic and adaptable method of adjudication. Seen in this light, the normative-empirical dichotomy could be justified by the theory of deep pockets and the policy of victim compensation, and it also appears to fit nicely with the ethos of broader liability that generally underpins the logic of enterprise liability.

Notably, this dichotomy also seems to be consistent with Judge Friendly's contextual approach in one of the leading US cases on enterprise liability, *Ira S Bushey and Sons Inc v United States*. There, he approved a passage from a leading treatise which suggested that 'what is reasonably foreseeable in [the context of vicarious liability]… is quite a different thing from the foreseeably unreasonable risk of harm that spells negligence'.[126] As such, it does not seem too much of a stretch to argue that the concept of inherent sporting risk ought to be subject to different methodologies (i.e. normative or empirical) depending on the legal question being asked (i.e. standard of care or vicarious liability).

The second concern relates to what might happen if the defendant produces empirical data to counteract the claimant's evidence that a particular harm was a reasonably foreseeable and frequent occurrence in that sport. In this instance, we might ponder why one view ought to be determinative. However, the courts have long had to deal with similar issues in the context of professional negligence, as illustrated by the so-called *Bolam* test (and the later *Bolitho* gloss that was applied to it).[127] It is rather common in medical negligence cases for judges to be faced with two competing sets of evidence; one body of expert opinion produced by the claimant (which will suggest that a doctor has not acted in accordance with an accepted practice) and one produced by the defendant (which, conversely, will seek to justify a particular act by reference to the similar practices of other doctors). Notably, the court will not determine the issue by deciding which body of opinion they prefer.[128] Rather, once the doctor is able to show that his acts are consistent with reasonable expert opinion, then 'the judge or jury *have* to accept' this evidence.[129]

A similar approach might work in the sporting context: once the claimant can demonstrate that a particular act was within the ordinary and expected risks of their sport, then the close connection test ought to be satisfied (regardless of any reasonable counter-evidence that might be produced by the defendant club). Of course, the *Bolitho* exception may still apply to the sporting context in order to ensure that a particular set of views are 'capable of withstanding logical analysis',[130] although it will likely be necessary in the future to clarify what criteria should lead a judge to find that a body of sporting opinion was unreasonable or irresponsible.[131]

Finally, an empirical, risk-based approach is perhaps open to the criticism that it may give rise to an inherently indeterminate method of adjudication. The risk of many on-field tortious acts could often be framed in various ways, with different permutations capable of leading to different empirical results. Consider, for instance, Morgan's suggestion that the result in *Gravil* would 'equally apply in a football context' because although 'violence may be more prevalent on-pitch with rugby… on-pitch violence in football is not unheard of'.[132] In this manner, he is able to conclude that 'on-pitch violence' is a 'reasonably incidental risk' of football. However, in assessing the relevance of *Gravil* to football, one might ponder whether the correct framing of the act ought merely to be 'violence' or, more specifically, 'punching'. If the latter, it is far more controversial to suggest that *Gravil* applies to the footballing context, as off-the-ball punching arguably occurs with much less frequency in football than it does in rugby union. It seems, then, that judicial rhetoric may be the primary factor influencing the determination of vicarious liability in this context.

This, however, is not particularly unusual (or even undesirable).[133] Judges have long been required, even under the traditional Salmond test, to determine how widely or narrowly a particular act ought to be characterised for the purposes of vicarious liability. Take the case of *London County Council v Cattermoles (Garages) Ltd*,[134] for example, where the issue for the Court of Appeal was whether the tortfeasor – who had been warned by his employer only to move cars out of a garage by hand – was acting in the course of employment when he negligently drove into the claimant's vehicle. Clearly, if the tortfeasor had only been employed to move cars *by hand*, then he was not acting within the course of employment according to the once-popular Salmond test. However, the court preferred a broader reading – according to which the tortfeasor was simply employed to move cars – which allowed them to find the defendant garage company vicariously liable for their employee's negligence.

A similar judicial determination will likely be required here, with judges having to decide, on the basis of both logic and consistency, how a particular on-field act ought to be framed. Deference to the normative intuitions of judges is, it seems, an inevitable by-product of adjudication in this area of law. As such, the empirical-normative dichotomy outlined above ought not to be rejected simply because it has the potential to produce uncertain results in practice.

Conclusion

It has been argued in this chapter that a more nuanced theoretical approach is required in order to adequately assess the appropriate scope of vicarious liability for on-the-field personal injuries. Attempting to draw a distinction between negligent and intentional acts is both unconvincing and inconsistent with recent case law, and it is a distinction that is perhaps best suited to the (now-outdated) era in which the Salmond test was utilised. Instead, I have argued that it would be desirable to focus our attention on the two dominant theoretical rationales that were identified and applied in *Gravil*: deterrence and enterprise liability.

In this regard, it was posited that the imposition of vicarious liability could provide one useful way of deterring violent on-field behaviour (particularly by those athletes who possess a reputation as an 'enforcer' or a 'hard man'). However, I also identified that there are several problems with relying solely on the deterrence rationale to justify vicarious liability. Whilst the *suitability argument* provides an ultimately unconvincing critique of deterrence, the *practicality argument* poses much greater difficulties for a deterrence-based approach. The deterrence of foul play is a rather speculative policy goal, and its illimitable boundaries would likely lead to vicarious liability for every tortious act committed on the field of play. In light of these points, it was suggested that deterrence alone could not operate as a satisfactory indicator of vicarious liability, and that it needed to be buttressed by another (arguably more dominant) theoretical rationale. This point was not considered by Clarke MR in *Gravil*, and he made no attempt to assess the relative weight that ought to be afforded to each theory in the context of on-the-field personal injury.

With this in mind, the chapter stressed the importance of adopting an enterprise liability-based approach for on-the-field acts. However, whilst there are many benefits to a risk-based assessment of vicarious liability in this context, it was highlighted that such an approach could clash with the normative analysis of a sport's playing culture that is conducted for the purposes of a negligence (or trespass) claim. This is a significant finding that has yet to be considered in any detail in most of the existing literature on this topic.

After considering several solutions to this so-called 'double-edged sword' problem – which included abandoning playing culture altogether, focussing more specifically on the benefit formulation of enterprise liability, and distinguishing between risk and the implied consent given by participants – it was concluded that we ought to draw an important distinction between the normative and empirical dimensions of inherent sporting risk. In this regard, whilst risk could be viewed in normative terms for the purposes of the standard of care enquiry, a more empirical conception of the inherent customs of a sport could be considered when assessing the scope of vicarious liability. This distinction could be justified by reference to the different policy bases that underpin both vicarious liability and the law on negligence. As such, and with this risk-based approach in mind, I now turn to analysing whether clubs could also be held vicariously liable for another type of harm that unfortunately occurs far too often on the sports field: discriminatory, race-based slurs.

Notes

1 See Mark James, 'Liability for Professional Athletes' Injuries: A Comparative Analysis of Where the Risk Lies' (2006) 1 Web JCLI.
2 [2002] 1 AC 215.
3 [2008] EWCA Civ 689.

4   See, e.g., *Elliott v Saunders and Liverpool FC* (unreported) High Court (QBD), 10 June 1994.
5   *Gravil* (n 3).
6   *Letang v Cooper* [1965] 1 QB 232, 239–40 (Lord Denning).
7   See, e.g., *KR and others v Royal and Sun Alliance Plc* [2006] EWCA Civ 1454.
8   *Condon v Basi* [1985] 1 WLR 866.
9   *Tylicki v Gibbons* [2021] EWHC 3470 (QB), [75] (HHJ Walden-Smith); *Caldwell v Maguire and Fitzgerald* [2001] EWCA Civ 1054, [28] (Tuckey LJ); *Elliott* (n 4), 9 (Drake J); *Wooldridge v Sumner* [1963] 2 QB 43, 67–8 (Diplock LJ).
10 *Caldwell* (n 9), [11].
11 Baroness Grey-Thompson, 'Duty of Care in Sport: Independent Report to Government' (Department for Digital, Culture, Media and Sport, April 2017) 26.
12 [2004] EWCA Civ 814, [21].
13 [1997] The Times, 11 February.
14 [1998] The Times, 26 November.
15 (unreported) County Court (Leeds), 15 January 1999.
16 Jack Anderson, *Modern Sports Law* (Hart 2010) 243. See also Simon Gardiner et al., *Sports Law* (4th edn, Routledge 2012) 505.
17 *Fulham Football Club v Mr Jordan Levi Jones* [2022] EWHC 1108 (QB); *Pitcher v Huddersfield Town Football Club* (2001) WL 753397; *Gaynor v Blackpool Football Club* [2002] CLY 3280.
18 [2012] UKSC 56, [62].
19 Mark James and David McArdle, 'Player Violence, or Violent Players? Vicarious Liability for Sports Participants' (2004) 12 Tort L Rev 131, 136.
20 Neville Cox, 'Civil Liability for Foul Play in Sport' (2003) 54 NILQ 351, 366–7.
21 Michael Beloff et al., *Sports Law* (2nd edn, Hart 2012) 157.
22 *Mohamud v WM Morrison Supermarkets plc* [2016] UKSC 11.
23 *Bellman v Northampton Recruitment Ltd* [2018] EWCA Civ 2214.
24 *Armes v Nottinghamshire County Council* [2017] UKSC 60.
25 *Racz v Home Office* [1994] 2 AC 45; *Makanjuola v Commissioner of Police for the Metropolis* [1989] 2 Admin LR 214.
26 JW Salmond, *Law of Torts* (Stevens and Haynes 1907) 83.
27 See, e.g., *Keppel Bus Co v Sa'ad bin Ahmad* [1974] 1 WLR 1082. However, cf *Poland v John Parr and Sons* [1927] 1 KB 236 and *Morris v Martin* [1966] 1 QB 716.
28 Robert Stevens, *Torts and Rights* (OUP 2007) 270. See also *New South Wales v Lepore* [2003] HCA 4, [117] (Gaudron J stating that it was a 'misuse of language' to say that deliberate criminal acts were committed within the course of employment).
29 *Lister* (n 2), [20], [67]. See, however, Paula Giliker, 'Vicarious Liability in the Common Law World: An Introduction' in Paula Giliker (ed), *Vicarious Liability in the Common Law World* (Hart 2022) 9 (noting that 'Salmond has proven hard to shift as an underlying test').
30 *Gravil* (n 3), [40].
31 ibid [26]–[8].
32 ibid [23].
33 ibid. Clarke MR was clearly convinced by the comments of Lord Steyn in *Bernard v Attorney General of Jamaica* [2004] UKPC 47, [19] (who had highlighted that 'an employer ought to be liable for a tort which can fairly be regarded as a reasonably incidental risk to the type of business he carried on').
34 Martha Chamallas, 'Vicarious Liability in Torts: The Sex Exception' (2013) 48 Val UL Rev 133, 138, 144–6.

35 Phillip Morgan, 'Distorting Vicarious Liability' (2011) 74 MLR 932, 934; Richard Epstein, *A Theory of Strict Liability: Toward a Reformulation of Tort Law* (Cato Institute 1980).
36 Other (comparative) examples include, in the US, *Atlanta Baseball v Lawrence*, 38 Ga. App. 497, 144 S.E. 351 (1928) and *Averill v Luttrell*, 44 Tenn. App. 56, 311 S.W.2d 812 (1957). For an Australian example, see *McCracken v Melbourne Storm Rugby League Club* [2005] NSWSC 107.
37 See generally, Jack Anderson, 'Violence, Sport and the Law: An Application to Gaelic Games' (1999) 7 Sport and the Law Journal 51.
38 Courtlyn Roser-Jones, 'A Costly Turnover: Why the NFL's Bounty Scandal Could Change the Current Legal Standard of Deferring to Internal Disciplinary Sanctions in Instances of Game-Related Violence' (2013) 20 Sports Lawyers Journal 93, 102.
39 *Gravil* (n 3), [2] (noting that Hughes LJ approved permission to appeal this case on the basis that 'the suggested liability for "off-the-ball" assaults committed during games is of sufficient potential importance for professional sporting clubs to provide a compelling reason for this court to entertain an appeal').
40 See, e.g., Neil Parpworth, 'Vicarious Liability on the Rugby Union Field' (2008) 172 Justice of the Peace 572; Jack Harris, 'A Sporting Chance' (2012) 162 NLJ 1248.
41 John Fleming, *The Law of Torts* (9th edn, LBC information Services 1998) 410.
42 *Gravil* (n 3), [26]–[7].
43 Anderson (n 16) 244. See also Philip Hutchinson, 'Who Shoulders the Blame? An Analysis of Vicarious Liability in the Sports Industry' (LawInSport, 03 October 2016); Mark James, *Sports Law* (3rd edn, Palgrave 2017) 87–8.
44 Parpworth (n 40); James (n 43) 95 (suggesting that a deterrence-based approach poses 'significant problems for clubs that employ a player with a known reputation for foul play, or one who over a period of time develops such a reputation whilst playing for a club, if steps are not taken to reduce the risk of the player harming others').
45 The primary role of a 'hard man' is to protect and motivate their teammates by intimidating the opposition. See, e.g., JCH Jones and Kenneth Stewart, 'Hit Somebody: Hockey Violence, Economics, the Law, and the *Twist* and *McSorley* Decisions' (2002) 12 Seton Hall J Sport L 165, 182.
46 James and McArdle (n 19) 142. See also James (n 43) 95 (arguing that, where a 'club is aware of such a [violent] tendency but ignores it, or otherwise fails to control, discipline or retrain the player, then... the club will be vicariously liable').
47 Phillip Morgan, 'Vicarious Liability and the Beautiful Game – Liability for Professional and Amateur Footballers?' (2018) 38 LS 242, 260.
48 ibid 248.
49 No. H-78–243 (S.D. Tex. Aug. 17, 1979).
50 Jeffrey Citron and Mark Ableman, 'Civil Liability in the Arena of Professional Sports' (2003) 36 UBC L Rev 193, 224.
51 For further exploration of this case, see Mark James, 'The Trouble with Roy Keane' (2002) 1 ESLJ 72, 87.
52 Nicholas McBride and Roderick Bagshaw, *Tort Law* (6th edn, Pearson 2018) 854.
53 Anthony Gray, *Vicarious Liability: Critique and Reform* (Hart 2018) 145–6; Gary Schwartz, 'Hidden and Fundamental Issue of Employer Vicarious Liability' (1996) 69 S Cal L Rev 1739, 1760; Jason Neyers and David Stevens, 'Vicarious Liability in the Charity Sector: An Examination of *Bazley v Curry* and *Re Christian Brothers of Ireland in Canada*' (2005) 42 CBLJ 371, 396.

54 Agnieszka McPeak, 'Sharing Tort Liability in the New Sharing Economy' (2016) 49 Conn L Rev 171, 192.
55 [2003] 1 WLR 2158.
56 ibid [9] (Judge LJ); [2002] EWHC 2177 (QB), [18] (HHJ Seymour).
57 ibid [33]–[4].
58 Paula Giliker, *Vicarious Liability in Tort: A Comparative Perspective* (CUP 2010) 170.
59 Gray (n 53) 51–2; Claire McIvor, 'The Use and Abuse of the Doctrine of Vicarious Liability' (2006) 35 CLWR 268, 280.
60 [1999] 2 SCR, [74]. See also *Viasystems (Tyneside) Ltd v Thermal Transfer (Northern) Ltd* [2005] EWCA Civ 1151, [55] (Rix LJ).
61 See generally, Simon Deakin, ''Enterprise-Risk: The Juridical Nature of the Firm Revisited' (2003) 32 ILJ 97; Guido Calabresi and Jon Hirschoff, 'Toward a Test for Strict Liability in Tort' (1972) 81 Yale LJ 1055.
62 Catherine Sharkey, 'Institutional Liability for Employees' Intentional Torts: Vicarious Liability as a Quasi-Substitute for Punitive Damages' (2018) 53 Val UL Rev 1, 5. To similar effect, see Williams Landes and Richard Posner, 'The Positive Economic Theory of Tort Law' (1981) 15 Ga L Rev 851, 904.
63 See, e.g., *Royal and Sun Alliance* (n 7).
64 Rob Merkin and Jenny Steele, *Insurance and the Law of Obligations* (OUP 2013) 319.
65 [2006] EWCA Civ 18. In other words, the vicarious nature of the employer's liability meant that, from their point of view, the bouncers' actions were in fact accidental. Had the employer's liability been personal, however, insurance cover would have been excluded because the injuries could not then have been viewed as 'accidental' from their perspective.
66 Fleming James and John Dickinson, 'Accident Proneness and Accident Law' (1950) 63 Harv L Rev 769, 781.
67 Patrick Atiyah, *Vicarious Liability in the Law of Torts* (Butterworths 1967) 17.
68 *Lepore* (n 28), [306].
69 ibid (Kirby J arguing that deterrence 'should be taken together' with a risk-based analysis).
70 Jason Neyers and Jerred Kiss, 'Vicarious Liability: The Revolution in Canada' in Paula Giliker (ed), *Vicarious Liability in the Common Law World* (Hart 2022) 38.
71 James Brown, 'Developing a Contextual-pluralist Model of Vicarious Liability' (2021) 28 Tort L Rev 123.
72 For a useful example of a judge analysing the weight of different theories, see *Barclays Bank plc v Various Claimants* [2018] EWCA Civ 1670, [56] (Irwin LJ referring to the theory of control as 'the most critical factor').
73 Howard Nixon, 'Accepting the Risks of Pain and Injury in Sport: Mediated Cultural Influences on Playing Hurt' (1993) 10 Sociology of Sport 183.
74 Gregory Keating, 'Distributive and Corrective Justice in the Tort Law of Accidents' (2000) 74 S Cal L Rev 193, 217.
75 *Graham v Commercial Bodyworks* [2015] EWCA Civ 47, [16] (Longmore LJ); McBride and Bagshaw (n 52) 845–7 (classifying cases which gives rise to foreseeable 'aggravations or annoyances' as 'special risk' cases, and citing *Gravil* as one such example).
76 *Armes* (n 24), [67] (Lord Reed).
77 See, e.g., Andrew Murray, Iain Murray and James Robson, 'Rugby Union: Faster, Higher, Stronger: Keeping an Evolving Sport Safe' (2014) 48 BJSM 73.
78 Alan Biggs, 'FIFA Ponders Red Card for Elbows' (*The Guardian*, 02 March 2007) <https://www.theguardian.com/football/2007/mar/02/newsstory.sport6>. For case law supporting this proposition, see *R v Blissett*, The Independent, 4th

December 1992 (where the former FA Chief executive, Graham Kelly, said that a raised elbow during an aerial duel was something that occurred at least 50 times per match).

79 Jones and Stewart (n 45) 181. See also Mark James and Simon Gardiner, 'Touch-lines and Guidelines: The Lord Advocate's Response to Sportsfield Violence' (1997) Crim L R 41, 44.

80 James (n 43) 91–2.

81 Patrick Murphy, John Williams and Eric Dunning, *Football on Trial: Spectator Violence and Development in the Football World* (Routledge 1990) 18.

82 Steve Greenfield et al., 'Reconceptualising the Standard of Care in Sport: The Case of Youth Rugby in England and South Africa' (2015) 18 PELJ 2184, 2199.

83 Glanville Williams, 'Consent and Public Policy' (1962) Crim L Rev 74, 81.

84 David McArdle and Mark James, 'Are you Experienced? Playing Cultures, Sporting Rules and Personal Injury Litigation after *Caldwell v Maguire*' (2005) 13 Tort L Rev 193, 198.

85 *Caldwell* (n 9), [12].

86 *R v Barnes* [2004] EWCA Crim 3246, [15] (Lord Woolf). See also John O'Brien, 'What Happens on the Field Stays on the Field? – Battery in Sport' (2015) 130 Precedent 23, 24 (outlining, for instance, that 'a player might reasonably expect certain contact in a game of rugby, whereas the same contact in a game of cricket might be highly objectionable').

87 Neil Tucker, 'Assumption of Risk and Vicarious Liability in Personal Injury Actions Brought by Professional Athletes' (1980) 1980 Duke LJ 742, 761.

88 ibid 762.

89 The analysis of the Colorado District Court in *Hackbart v Cincinnati Bengals Inc.* 435 F. Supp. 352, p.356 (D. Colo. 1977) – which was later overruled by the United States Court of Appeals for the Tenth Circuit – appears to support this proposition.

90 James and McArdle (n 19) 138–9.

91 Tucker (n 87) 762.

92 Edward Grayson, *Sport and the Law*, (2nd edn, Butterworths 1994) 157; Alexandra-Virgil Voicu, 'Civil Liability Arising from Breaches of Sports Regulations' (2005) 1 ISLJ 22, 22–3.

93 Curtis Fogel, 'Ultra-Violence on the Pitch: Establishing a Threshold for the Intervention of Criminal Law in English Football' (2014) 2 JLCJ 11, 24. For a similar view outlining the importance of playing culture, see David McArdle, *From Boot Money to Bosman: Football, Society and the Law* (Cavendish 2000) 158.

94 *Czernuszka v King* [2023] EWHC 380 (KB), [43] (Spencer J); *Fulham* (n 17), [63] (Lane J).

95 [2014] CSOH 100, [216] [emphasis added].

96 *Gravil* (n 3), [36].

97 ibid.

98 Notable 'masters of the dark arts' in football include Pepe, Sergio Ramos and Diego Costa. In regards to the latter, see Barney Ronay, 'Chelsea's Diego Costa Leaves No Evidence after the Perfect Heist' (*The Guardian*, 19 September 2015) <https://www.theguardian.com/football/blog/2015/sep/19/chelsea-diego-costa-evidence-heist-arsenal> (referring to an incident in which Costa 'deliberately and skilfully got an opponent sent off... [and this] effectively won the game for his team').

99 Steven Rubin, 'The Vicarious Liability of Professional Sports Teams for On-the-Field Assaults Committed by their Players' (1999) 1 Va J Sports & L 266, 285.

100 [2016] UKSC 10, [30].

101 George Priest, 'The Invention of Enterprise Liability: A Critical History of the Intellectual Foundations of Modern Tort Law' (1985) 14 JLS 461, 527.
102 *Blake* (n 12).
103 McArdle and James (n 84) 6; O'Brien (n 86) 25–6.
104 Allan Beever, *Rediscovering the Law of Negligence* (Hart 2007) 349.
105 [1971] 2 QB 691, 701.
106 Adam Pendlebury, 'Perceptions of Playing Culture in Sport: The Problem of Diverse Opinion in the Light of *Barnes*' (2006) 4 ESLJ 1, 4.
107 Simon Deakin and Zoe Adams, *Markesinis and Deakin's Tort Law* (8th edn, OUP 2019) 764.
108 Pendlebury (n 106) 4–5.
109 ibid 5.
110 ibid.
111 *Barnes* (n 86), [15].
112 [1978] Crim LR 553.
113 ibid 553. The quote, which the defendant sought to rely on, came from Mervyn Davies, a former Welsh international rugby union player. Note also the comments of Simon Devereux (from *R v Devereux*, The Independent, 23 February 1996) who, after being released early from his 9-month imprisonment for on-field assault, stated that his 'flare-up' was 'no different to countless others on rugby pitches the length and breadth of Britain every Saturday of the season'. See Anderson (n 16) 196.
114 Pendlebury (n 106) 4.
115 I have only been able to identify two works that delve into an empirical assessment of a sport's inherent risks: Pendlebury (n 106); Curtis Fogel, *Game-Day Gangsters: Crime and Deviance in Canadian Football* (Athabasca University Press 2013) 31–56.
116 *Canterbury Bankstown Rugby League Football Club v Rogers* [1993] Aust Tort Reports 81–246.
117 See, e.g., the alleged pre-meditated plan by the Vancouver Canucks NHL team to target Colorado Avalanche's Steve Moore in a 2004 game: *R v Bertuzzi* [2004] BCPC 472.
118 National Football League, 'NFL Says Saints Created "Bounty" Program from 2009 to 2011' (*NFL*, 02 March 2012) <https://www.nfl.com/news/nfl-says-saints-created-bounty-program-from-2009-to-2011–09000d5d82757bcd>.
119 McArdle (n 93) 168.
120 See, e.g., the hit-list created by the Green Bay Packers' Charles Martin in 1973, when he was reported to have the numbers of five opposition players he sought to injure written on a towel and tucked into his waist. This story is outlined in more detail by Roser-Jones (n 38) 104.
121 Associated Press, 'Cris Carter Admits to Bounties' (*ESPN*, 09 May 2012) <https://www.espn.co.uk/nfl/story/_/id/7907610/cris-carter-formerly-minnesota-vikings-admits-authorizing-bounties>.
122 Patrick Hruby, 'New Orleans Saints Bounty is Just A Part of the Game' (*The Guardian*, 05 March 2012) <https://www.theguardian.com/sport/blog/2012/mar/05/nfl-bounty-new-orleans-saints-brett-favre>.
123 Simon Evans, 'Redskins Players Also Had "Bounty" System: Reports' (*Reuters*, 03 March 2012) <https://www.reuters.com/article/us-nfl-bounty-idUSTRE8220TW20120303>.
124 Anderson (n 16) 196. See also Barbara Hink, 'Compensating Injured Professional Athletes: The Mystique of Sport Versus Traditional Tort Principles' (1980) 55 New York University Law Review 971, 989; Jack Anderson, 'No Licence

for Thuggery: Violence, Sport and the Criminal Law' (2008) 10 Criminal Law Review 751, 761.

125 *R v Lloyd* (1989) 11 Cr App R(S) 36, 37 (Pill J).
126 398 F 2d 167, 171 (2nd Cir, 1968), quoting Fowler Harper and Fleming James, *Law of Torts* (Little Brown & Co 1956) 1372.
127 *Bolam v Friern Hospital Management Committee* [1957] 1 WLR 582; *Bolitho v City and Hackney Health Authority* [1998] AC 232.
128 *Maynard v West Midlands Regional Health Authority* [1984] 1 WLR 634, 648 (Lord Scarman); *Sidaway v Governors of Bethlem Royal Hospital* [1985] AC 871, 895 (Lord Diplock).
129 *Adams v Rhymney Valley DC* [2000] Lloyd's Rep PN 777, [41] (emphasis added).
130 *Bolitho* (n 127) 243 (Lord Browne-Wilkinson).
131 For now, the seven-point guidance on the relevant *Bolitho* factors outlined by Mulheron may be particularly instructive. See Rachel Mulheron, 'Trumping *Bolam*: A Critical Legal Analysis of *Bolitho's* "Gloss"' (2010) 69 CLJ 609.
132 Morgan (n 47) 247–8.
133 In fact, and as I explore in Brown (n 71) 133, judges are required to confront similar issues in legal causation cases.
134 [1953] 1 WLR 997.

3 Vicarious Liability for On-the-Field Acts

Responding to Racism

Introduction

Building on the theory of risk that was utilised in the previous chapter, this chapter recognises that broken bones and torn tendons are not the only harms that might occur in a fast-paced, competitive sporting contest. In fact, other (often more insidious) harms also occur on the field of play. We are talking here, of course, about discriminatory comments or gestures made by one player to another. This chapter examines whether vicarious liability can – and indeed should – be imposed on a club for such conduct. Whilst it is true that discriminatory behaviour in sport may take place away from the field between members of the same team, the focus in this chapter will be on the appropriate scope of vicarious liability for on-the-field comments made by an individual against an opposition player. That said, certain examples of internal, off-the-field discrimination between teammates will be briefly discussed in order to highlight how the institutionally racist nature of many sports clubs could feed into an analysis of the close connection test in this context. Furthermore, and mostly for purposes of space, the focus in this chapter will predominantly be on racial discrimination. However, much of this analysis could equally apply to other forms of discrimination in sport (such as, for instance, homophobic abuse).[1]

With this in mind, the chapter begins by illustrating how insights from Critical Race Theory ('CRT') could be used to inform an enterprise liability-based approach to discriminatory harms. In particular, I suggest that an interdisciplinary approach to vicarious liability – which draws on a variety of less conventional, non-legal theories and concepts – may provide a useful method for enriching the more traditional rationales for the doctrine. This is demonstrated by drawing on a legal realist conception of law. This discussion concludes by highlighting that the imposition of vicarious liability may be necessary in order to expose the fact that institutional racism is a significant problem within many sporting enterprises.

Thereafter, the chapter explores three potential legal options that may be used to hold a club vicariously liable for racial discrimination perpetrated on

DOI: 10.4324/9781032665870-3

the sports field. These include: vicarious liability for a common law tort (such as negligence, trespass to the person or the tort in *Wilkinson v Downton*); statutory vicarious liability (under s.109 of the Equality Act 2010); and common law vicarious liability for breach of a statutory duty (under the Protection from Harassment Act 1997). This chapter maintains that none of these options are entirely satisfactory, and it suggests that there is a significant gap in the law when looking at an employer's vicarious responsibility for racist conduct by one of their employees. Consequently, I examine the possibility of introducing a new (potentially sport-specific) tort of hate speech to deal with such behaviour. In contrast to some scholars who have suggested a similar development, I argue that the wrong in racist slurs ought to be more appropriately based in anti-discrimination law (and its concomitant commitment to egalitarianism) rather than in the law on harassment. Finally, the chapter concludes by offering a few justifications for potentially limiting this new tort to the on-field sporting context.

Racial Abuse in Sport: Insights from Critical Race Theory

According to recent statistics released by the Home Office, football-related hate crime remains one of the most reported incidents at live matches.[2] Of these incidents, almost 75% related to race during the 2021–22 season.[3] Such evidence appears to reinforce the sentiments of various scholars such as Williams who have described sport as a 'racially polluted' working environment.[4] As Cleland and Cashmore further elaborate, the game continues to operate as a predominantly white institution, particularly in relation to those individuals – such as club owners, directors and heads of governing bodies – that assume responsibility for the governance of the sport.[5] Consequently, racist behaviour on matchdays is unfortunately an all-too-common occurrence.

Although it is fair to say that most racist abuse in sport now comes from the terraces or 'fan-made' social media accounts,[6] racial slurs are also sometimes uttered by the participants themselves. Luis Suarez, for example, was adjudged to have racially abused Manchester United defender Patrice Evra during a game in 2011,[7] and in the same season, the Football Association also punished Chelsea captain John Terry for directing the words 'fucking black cunt' towards opposition defender Anton Ferdinand.[8] Likewise, an amateur Welsh rugby-union player was banned for eight weeks in 2020 after using a racial slur against an opponent, an example which highlights that racism can trickle down even to the grassroots level.[9] Sports such as ice hockey,[10] cricket[11] and Australian-rules football[12] have also had to contend with numerous instances of discriminatory on-field comments made by athletes.

It is this state of affairs that has led some scholars to employ theoretical methodologies such as Critical Race Theory (CRT) in an attempt to respond to this sort of heinous behaviour. CRT is a subset of Critical Legal Studies (CLS),[13] an intellectual movement which suggests that the law is infused with political ideals and 'filled with gaps and contradictions'.[14] However, there is a crucial difference between CRT and CLS. Whilst it is true that both concepts seek to mount a 'full frontal assault on the edifice of modern jurisprudence',[15] Ladson-Billings outlines that race-related issues are only on the periphery of CLS's critique of societal power structures. In contrast, she explains, CRT brings such issues to the fore by centralising the discussion of racism.[16] On this basis, and as Hylton describes in the context of sport, CRT acts as a 'framework from which to explore and examine the racism in society that privileges whiteness as it disadvantages others because of their "blackness"'.[17]

It is suggested that there are two overlapping ways in which CRT is relevant to the analysis in this book. First, it highlights the benefits of a truly interdisciplinary approach to the doctrine of vicarious liability. Second, it also demonstrates that some of the more traditional rationales of vicarious liability – such as, for example, enterprise risk – can be enriched by insights from other (less conventional) theories and concepts.

Interdisciplinarity and the Limits of 'Legal' Research

The first benefit of considering CRT in this chapter is that it neatly illustrates the importance of a more interdisciplinary approach to vicarious liability. As Hylton opines, CRT is a 'hybrid discipline as it draws from a number of necessarily relevant disciplines to incorporate a transdisciplinary approach to the development of theory... in relation to racism in society'.[18] As such, it can incorporate a wide range of perspectives – such as legal, humanities and social science research – as part of its analytical and empirical framework. This is reinforced by the fact that CRT appears to be grounded in the school of thought known as legal realism.[19] Proponents of this approach view law in functional terms as a means to an end, and they are keen to stress the importance of embedding 'social consciousness' into legal judgments.[20] The close methodological ties between CRT and legal realism have even led some to advance a new form of 'Critical Race Realism',[21] a concept which seeks to ensure that judicial decision-making is more attentive to 'the social facts upon which law must proceed and to which law must be applied'.[22] As such, CRT may be open to insight from a wide array of scholarship: sociology, psychology, history, economics, political science etc.

Given its overtly hybrid nature, some are likely to question whether CRT is really an appropriate tool for analysing the scope of the close connection test. After all, many are likely to see this as a purely 'legal' question.[23] However, I argue that we should not be oblivious to how other (less conventional) frameworks and ideologies could help us to apply the theories of vicarious liability in certain contexts. Indeed, if a certain methodology leads us to a better or more informed decision, it should not be ignored solely on the basis that it was derived from a "non-legal" source. As Priel claims, there ought to be 'no limitation on lawyers or judges relying on relevant information, from whatever "knowledge discipline", for the sake of maintaining law as an academic discipline'.[24] In his view:

> Truths about the world are not themselves 'legal', 'chemical', 'economic', or 'psychological': These are human categories imposed upon reality that itself does not contain them... the content of our law should be based on truths. If a truth is *relevant* to making a better decision, it matters little whether they have been arrived at using 'lawyers' methods' or by other means.[25]

It is perhaps worth remembering, then, that legal rules and theories are what Harari refers to as 'inter-subjective', and they only exist within the shared consciousness of humanity.[26] Accordingly, if enough people believe that this 'imagined order' of theoretical rationales can be improved by adopting an interdisciplinary approach, then change can – and indeed should – occur.

In order to further conceptualise this point, it is worth returning to the notion of legal realism that underpins much of the analysis in this book. Under Dagan's 'reconstructed realist conception',[27] he perceives law as being fuelled by (amongst other things) a tension between tradition and progress.[28] In his view, the 'realist approach seeks to open up a space for a forward-looking perspective within law's respect for tradition'.[29] Llewellyn appears to make a similar point in his earlier work when he suggests that a 're-examination and reworking of the heritage' may be one useful step to take in aiming to fulfil our quest for 'better and best law'.[30]

This tension between tradition and progress could, I suggest, be mapped on to the interdisciplinary approach advocated in this chapter: whilst I wish to respect and maintain the more traditional rationales for vicarious liability, I equally recognise that, in some instances, these rationales could be supported and enhanced by other interdisciplinary concepts. In turn, this could lead to more desirable results in practice. Of course, though, striking an appropriate balance between tradition and progress is never likely to be an easy task, and it is for such reasons that I seek to illustrate in later chapters how feminist legal theory and masculinities studies could be employed to enrich an enterprise liability-based approach to off-the-field sexual abuse by athletes. For now, however, it is worth examining how CRT could be utilised to help enhance the theory of risk under this tradition-progress dichotomy.

Enterprise Risk and Critical Race Theory

The argument made in this section is that, by adopting a 'race-based systematic critique of... legal institutions',[31] CRT could be employed to intellectually enhance an enterprise liability-based analysis of racist on-the-field

conduct. By recognising the failures of many sporting institutions to suffi-
ciently address racial inequality, it could be that CRT sits rather neatly alongside a risk-based approach to vicarious liability, in that it 'captures the causal
role the employer plays in creating or facilitating the harm'.[32] Indeed, shifting
liability on to clubs may help to send out the symbolic message that racism
is an institutional problem within many clubs across a wide range of sports,
rather than just a problem that is created (and perpetuated) by a few 'bad
apples' in the sporting community. After all, and as Hall outlines, 'framing
the abuser as [an] outsider, somehow "slipping through the cracks", fooling
the gatekeepers with diabolical duplicity, is a very workable model, from the
institutional perspective'.[33] CRT exposes this fallacy, and helps to highlight
that racism may be a far more systemic problem than most clubs would care
to admit.

Consider, for instance, the allegations of 'widespread and deep-rooted racism' in English cricket.[34] A recent report from the Independent Commission
for Equity in Cricket – which drew on the lived experiences of 4,156 individuals involved in the sport – highlighted that racism is a 'serious issue' in
cricket.[35] The Commission observed that 'racism in cricket is not about "a
few bad apples" or limited to individual incidents of misconduct'.[36] Rather,
it is a systemic problem that continues to plague the sport as a whole. 'Bad
apples', the Commission continued, 'do not exist in isolation, separate from
everyone else: they are part of the cricket community and left unchecked, can
infect the rest'.[37]

This report was issued in the wake of the testimony provided by Azeem
Rafiq to the Digital, Culture, Media and Sport ('DCMS') committee. In it, he
accused his former employer, the Yorkshire County Cricket Club ('YCCC'),
of being 'institutionally racist'.[38] It was reported that Rafiq and a number
of other Asian players at the club were regularly referred to as 'Paki's' and
'elephant washers',[39] and that YCCC had swept this toxic atmosphere under
the rug by labelling it as 'friendly and good-natured banter'.[40] Similar stories of abuse are also told by those cricketers who played for Essex County
Cricket Club during their career. Zoheb Sharif, for instance, revealed that
his Essex teammates used to refer to him as 'bomber' and 'curry muncher',
whilst Jamaican-born Maurice Chambers was also taunted by having bananas
thrown at him.[41] As such, it is perhaps little surprise that, in the Commission's
report, 87% of respondents with Pakistani and Bangladeshi heritage (as well
as 82% of people with Indian heritage, and 75% of Black respondents) experienced some form of discrimination within cricket.[42]

Cricket is not, of course, the only sport to be plagued by allegations of
institutional racism. For example, the successful Australian-rules football
team, Collingwood, was said to have a culture of 'systemic racism' that
was due, in large part, to the club's 'deny, double-down and deflect' response to racist behaviour.[43] Similarly, in the context of football, Burdsey

has recently contended that racism is firmly rooted in the sport's institutions and structures.[44] Interestingly, he also notes that the belief that football is now a colour-blind industry free from racist attitudes actually enables racism to insidiously operate in more 'complex, nuanced and often covert ways that go under the radar of football authorities and beyond the capacities of anti-racist groups'.[45] It may be necessary, therefore, to impose vicarious liability on clubs to help us transparently expose the wisdom that CRT urges us to uncover: that institutional racism continues to plague many professional clubs in a variety of sports. After all, and as Kenney highlights, holding clubs strictly liable for racist slurs might help to 'send a strong signal to fans, players and coaches that... [sport] is finally ready to fight' the scourge of discriminatory abuse.[46]

Before assessing the potential legal remedies available to a claimant who has been subjected to racial abuse on the field, it is perhaps worth mentioning an important final caveat that CRT arguably overlooks: imposing vicarious liability on sports clubs may only be appropriate if it can be established that sport increases the risk of racist behaviour over-and-above the background risk of racism in society. After all, the more the risk is enhanced due to the existence of the club, the fairer it arguably becomes to impose vicarious liability. Now, it must be recognised that identifying (and comparing) such a background risk is likely to be very difficult in practice. For such reasons, and as I explore in more detail in the next chapter, it seems reasonable to conclude that vicarious liability is justified so long as a club's toxic culture makes a 'material contribution' to any racist abuse. In light of the examples mentioned above, this may not prove to be an overly difficult task for many athletes in a variety of sports.

Vicarious Liability for On-the-Field Racism: Potential Causes of Action

The previous section argued that the interdisciplinary concept of CRT could be used to help establish that racist behaviour is oftentimes a systemic problem within many sporting institutions. As such, the imposition of vicarious liability on clubs may be necessary in order to expose the fact that the risk of racial abuse is frequently facilitated (and perhaps even created) by sports clubs. However, as this section seeks to demonstrate, it might be very difficult to establish the liability of an employer for such conduct. This is due to the fact that there is seemingly no obvious tort upon which to hinge the vicarious liability of a club. Whilst the criminal law is able to deal with on-the-field racism in a rather effective manner,[47] there appears to be a significant gap when we examine the response of the civil law to this issue. This can be illustrated by assessing the following three options that are available to a claimant who wishes to establish the vicarious liability of their wrongdoer's club.

Vicarious Liability for Common Law Torts: Negligence, the Rule in Wilkinson v Downton and Trespass to the Person

The first option for a sports claimant who is pursuing a vicarious liability claim is to establish that the perpetrator of the racist abuse is liable in negligence. The tort of negligence is perhaps the most common tort that is relied upon in order to impose vicarious liability on an employer. However, it is unlikely that negligence could be established for racist on-the-field comments. This is not because of any difficulties in proving a breach of duty, but rather because the tort of negligence requires a claimant to show that they have suffered a recognisable physical or psychological injury.

Importantly, this is also the case for the so-called *Wilkinson v Downton* tort which is concerned with the intentional infliction of emotional harm.[48] As the Supreme Court confirmed in *O (a child) v Rhodes*, the claimant must have suffered 'physical harm or [a] recognised psychiatric illness' in order to claim under the rule in *Wilkinson v Downton*.[49] Whilst it would be perhaps too hasty to suggest that discriminatory abuse between sports participants could *never* reach this threshold, it must be recognised that, in most instances, racial slurs would not lead to this high degree of harm.

Likewise, trespass to the person is unlikely to be of much use to a claimant either. Trespass to the person encapsulates the torts of assault and battery, so unless a racist remark is accompanied by a physical attack (or at least a threat to attack), then the claimant will not have a remedy under this cause of action. Of course, in certain instances, racist behaviour may coincide with some form of unwanted physical contact. For instance, as part of his written evidence submitted to the DCMS, Azeem Rafiq claimed that fellow cricketer Alex Morris pinned him down and forced him to drink red wine.[50] As a practicing Muslim at the time, Rafiq did not drink alcohol, and this would be a clear battery. Similarly, in a non-sporting context, *Mohamud v Wm Morrison Supermarkets plc* provides another good example of racist language that was accompanied by a physical attack.[51] In that case, a Morrisons employee hurled racist abuse at a customer before following him onto a petrol station forecourt and attacking him. In practice, however, such incidents are likely to be rare when dealing with racism that is perpetrated on the sports field.

Statutory Vicarious Liability: Equality Act 2010

The second possible way to establish the vicarious liability of a club for racism is to rely on the protection afforded under the Equality Act 2010 ('EA 2010'). Racial discrimination in sport is typically covered by harassment under s.26 EA 2010. This provision highlights that an individual will commit harassment if they engage in 'unwanted conduct related to a relevant protected characteristic', and that conduct either violates another party's dignity or creates an 'intimidating, hostile, degrading, humiliating or offensive environment' for that person. Importantly, and as demonstrated by s.109 EA 2010, such conduct could also lead to the liability of the wrongdoer's employer if it is done in the course of employment. A useful case example to illustrate this point is that of *Hussaney v Chester City FC and Kevin Ratcliffe*.[52] Here, the claimant, a reserve professional football player, successfully argued that he had been the victim of racial discrimination after his first-team manager called him a 'black cunt'. The claimant was awarded £2,500 for injury to his feelings, and the club were subsequently held vicariously liable for the manager's racist outburst.[53]

There are, however, two major problems with relying on statutory vicarious liability under s.109 EA 2010. First, the EA 2010 is designed to protect individuals from discrimination within their own workplace. In other words, it operates internally between employees of the same organisation.[54] As such, whilst it would be a useful tool for athletes such as Rafiq to rely on,[55] the EA 2010 provides a rather unsatisfactory remedy for the type of behaviour that this chapter focusses on: racist conduct *on the sports field*. In the vast majority of cases, on-the-field discrimination will be perpetrated by one player against a member of the opposition (rather than against their own teammate).[56] Consequently, the only way that the EA 2010 could be relevant for on-the-field conduct is if another player from the wrongdoer's club overhears the comments, and subsequently commences an action. The fact that the comments are not specifically directed at their own teammate would not prevent them from making a claim. This scenario is, however, likely to be very rare in practice.

Second, even if the EA 2010 could be triggered for racism on the sports field, s.109 may not provide an entirely effective method of imposing vicarious liability on the wrongdoer's club. This is evidenced by s.109(4) EA 2010, which highlights that an employer can defend themselves against liability by demonstrating that they 'took all reasonable steps' to prevent their employee from committing a wrongful act. The problem with this provision, however, is that it does not really give rise to *vicarious* liability. By introducing an element of fault into this defence, s.109 EA 2010 embodies primary liability rather than (strict) vicarious liability.

This is reinforced by the fact that s.109(1) treats an employee's discriminatory act as one also done by their employer. This harks back to the now-outdated 'master's tort' theory of vicarious liability, which views the wrongful act as being committed by the master (or employer) rather than by the employee.[57] This theory is now considered somewhat unfashionable, and it has been criticised for introducing an element of fault into a doctrine of strict liability.[58] Indeed, a fault-based conception of liability for racist conduct may also be somewhat antithetical to the ethos of broader liability that appears to underpin enterprise liability. Although courts have recently confirmed that employers need to do more than simply implement an equality policy to avail themselves of the 'reasonable steps' defence,[59] the fact-specific nature of s.109 means that employer liability for racist conduct is undoubtedly narrower under the EA 2010 than it would be for true (strict) vicarious liability.

Common Law Vicarious Liability for Breach of a Statutory Duty: Protection from Harassment Act 1997

Unlike the EA 2010, liability under the Protection from Harassment Act 1997 ('PHA 1997') is not contingent upon whether an employer has taken reasonable steps to prevent the harm. As such, and as Stevens recognises, liability here espouses the more conventional 'servant's tort' theory of vicarious liability, which views the doctrine as imposing liability on one party (typically an employer) for the wrongful acts of another (typically an employee).[60]

Following *Majrowski v Guy's and St Thomas's NHS Trust* – a case which concerned a clinical audit co-ordinator for an NHS trust successfully alleging that he had been harassed by his departmental manager – it has now been confirmed that an employer can be vicariously liable for the statutory tort of harassment under s.3 PHA 1997.[61] In apparent consonance with the earlier view of Atiyah,[62] Auld LJ in the Court of Appeal maintained that it is 'immaterial whether the conduct in respect of which a claimant seeks to hold an employer to account is a breach of a common law or statutory duty'.[63] The House of Lords agreed and added that, unless a statutory provision explicitly or impliedly excludes an employer's liability, then vicarious liability can arise (provided that the relevant act is done within the course of employment).[64] Notably, there seems to be no limitation on the ability of non-employee third parties to recover under this provision, such that it is perhaps more appropriate to deal with on-the-field racist abuse between opponents under the PHA 1997, rather than under the EA 2010.

In the case of *Majrowski* itself, the justification for finding a close connection was premised primarily on enterprise risk-based reasoning, in that harassment was said to be an inherent risk of the claimant's working environment. As Auld LJ explained, the workplace is the 'very place where harassment is often encountered and from which its victim is often powerless to escape. It is thus often likely to be a risk incidental to employment'.[65] Seen in this light, it may be relatively easy to conclude that racial abuse is an incidental risk of many sports. A close connection could be predicated, for instance, on the fact that on-the-field discriminatory abuse is part and parcel of the game, because it constitutes little more than a 'cynical and calculated act of "gamesmanship" to wind up an opposing player'.[66]

Alternatively, and with one eye on the important lessons that were gleaned from CRT in the previous section, a close connection could also be established on the basis of the prevailing white hegemony that is embedded into the fabric of many sports. We have already seen, for instance, that football has been described as a 'racially polluted' working environment.[67] Likewise, and in light of the aforementioned institutional racism in English cricket, it would not be a particularly controversial development to hold a cricket club vicariously liable under the PHA 1997 for on-the-field racist language used by one of their players.

The real issue lies, it seems, in determining whether the tort of harassment could be made out in the first place. As is made clear under s.1 PHA 1997, harassment is committed if a person pursues a 'course of conduct' that is both oppressive and unreasonable,[68] and which the perpetrator 'knows or ought to know amounts to harassment of the other'. Whilst it was recognised by Baroness Hale in *Majrowski* that 'a great deal is left to the wisdom of the courts to draw sensible lines between the ordinary banter and badinage of life and genuinely offensive and unacceptable behaviour',[69] it seems likely that most on-the-field racial slurs go beyond mere 'irritations' or 'annoyances',[70] and thus satisfy the necessary threshold of seriousness required for liability under the PHA 1997. This is reinforced by the fact that such abuse, as demonstrated in *R v Terry*, could trigger criminal liability under s.2.[71]

The obvious stumbling block in establishing liability for on-the-field harassment is the need to show that the perpetrator engaged in a 'course of conduct'. Unlike under the EA 2010, a solitary act cannot constitute harassment under the PHA 1997; a claimant must show that such conduct has occurred on at least two separate occasions.[72] Although this would not necessarily pose a problem in relation to Evra's claim against Suarez (given the finding that the former was called a 'negro' seven times during the course of the game),[73] it will generally be the case that racist remarks are only uttered once during the period of play. In light of Lord Hoffmann's sentiments in *Wainwright v Home Office* – where he suggested that it would not be 'in the public interest to allow the law to be set in motion for one boorish incident'[74] – it must be concluded that the PHA 1997 also fails to provide a satisfactory remedy for most instances of on-the-field racial abuse between two opposing players.

Time for a Sport-Specific Tort of Hate Speech?

The previous section argued that the three potential remedies available to a claimant who has suffered on-the-field racial abuse all have fundamental limitations. As such, the law in this area appears to lack an effective and appropriate tort upon which to hinge the vicarious liability of a club. If we are to implement CRT's political ambitions for change, then it is perhaps worth considering whether we can develop a simpler route for holding clubs strictly liable for on-the-field racial slurs. The argument propounded in this section is that it may be wise to create a new (potentially sport-specific) tort of hate speech that could be used to respond to such conduct.

To be clear, this is not an entirely novel suggestion. Scholars have already recommended that the law on harassment be reformed so that a 'course of conduct' is no longer required. For instance, Gardiner and Welch have suggested that:

> [i]t would be preferable to develop the law [on harassment] so that even a single act of racist (or homophobic etc.) abuse could constitute a new tort

(civil wrong) of racial harassment so that the opposing player's club could then be rendered legally responsible for any racist behaviour by one or more of its players during a match.[75]

In sum, Gardiner and Welch appear to be translating what is, in effect, a public order offence into an actionable tort. This is to be welcomed. As Len and Ruijter opine, 'private litigation gives targets of hate speech control over the narrative and explication of harm that lies at the heart of a civil dispute in ways that criminal or administrative legal tools do not'.[76] That said, however, I do believe that Gardiner and Welch's solution should be subject to two clarificatory points. First, the gist of the wrong in cases of racial slurs ought to be based in discrimination rather than harassment. Second, the implementation of a new tort for racial slurs could, at least for the time being, be limited specifically to the sporting context. Let us now unpack these two arguments in more detail in order to demonstrate how a sport-specific tort of hate speech might be able to finally provide an effective mechanism for holding clubs vicariously liable for racist on-the-field behaviour.

Racist Slurs as a Civil Wrong: Discrimination or Harassment?

A new tort to combat racial insults is better viewed as an anti-discrimination provision rather than a law designed to protect people from harassment. As such, rather than referring to a modification of the tort of harassment (as Gardiner and Welch appear to do), it may be wise to use a more appropriate, anti-discrimination-focussed, name for this new tort: the 'tort of hate speech'. Richard Delgado, one of the pioneers of CRT, advocated for a similar development back in 1982 when he suggested that we ought to develop a new free-standing tort for insults that are 'intended to demean through reference to race'.[77] In his view:

> An independent tort for racial slurs would protect the interests of personality and equal citizenship that are part of our highest political traditions and moral values, thereby affirming the right of all citizens to lead their lives free from attacks on their dignity and psychological integrity.[78]

Interestingly, however, Delgado makes no reference to harassment when developing this new tort, and this is perhaps for good reason: harassment laws, such as the PHA 1997, are primarily designed to respond to the threat of stalking, bullying and other forms of anti-social behaviour.[79] In contrast, the underlying policy of anti-discrimination laws is to eliminate inequality in society, and this is more in line with the political aspirations of CRT. Indeed, anti-discrimination laws often tend to be described as 'equality laws',[80] and Collins observes that the main (distributive) aim of such laws is to promote 'social inclusion'.[81] As such, the policy goal of anti-discrimination seems to be a much more appropriate hook upon which to hinge the vicarious liability of a club for racism than the protection from harassment.

This is seemingly reinforced by Gardiner and Riches' point, as they argue that anti-discrimination laws 'function as a means to say something... and, therefore, operate in a symbolic manner'.[82] In this light, and in drawing upon the work of Sunstein,[83] we might conclude that a new tort of hate speech embodies a normative statement designed to express and shift social norms on discrimination. Shifting these wider social norms would be far more difficult if a new tort was to be based in harassment (which, as we have seen, is arguably more concerned with regulating relationships between individuals than it is with broader societal goals).

The unique policy goal of anti-discrimination laws is also evidenced, I believe, by the distinction that is drawn by some judges between statutory vicarious liability under the EA 2010 and vicarious liability at common law. For instance, Waite LJ in *Jones v Tower Boot Co* argued that the course of employment test in the statutory context should be considered 'with a mind unclouded by any parallels sought to be drawn from the law of vicarious liability in tort'.[84] In recognising the unique purpose served by anti-discrimination laws, His Lordship suggested that it would be wrong to apply:

> a common law principle evolved in another area of the law to deal with vicarious responsibility for wrongdoing of a wholly different kind. To do so would seriously undermine the statutory scheme of the discrimination Acts and flout the purposes which they were passed to achieve.[85]

As such, if a new tort of hate speech is to be created, it may be worth considering whether a more contextualised and policy-driven application of the close connection test would be appropriate when applying vicarious liability for this tort. If a new tort of hate speech serves a different policy goal rooted in equality and symbolism, then it may be legitimate (and indeed normatively desirable) to modify the close connection test when applying the doctrine of vicarious liability for this tort. Whether, of course, this is likely to receive judicial acceptance is a matter of some doubt, particularly as the Supreme Court in *Trustees of the Barry Congregation of Jehovah's Witnesses v BXB* has recently rejected the idea that the law on vicarious liability needs to be tailored in certain contexts (e.g. in sexual abuse cases).[86]

A Sport-Specific Remedy?

The second, and arguably more controversial, clarification of Gardiner and Welch's suggestion is to limit it specifically to the on-field sporting context. This would be controversial because it would appear to provide greater protection from discrimination to the (financially) privileged in society. Many would likely question why a famous athlete from a minority background would be able to rely on the tort, but any other individual from a similar background would be afforded no remedy at all. Even though I would have no objection to extending the tort of hate speech to all contexts, there may be two good reasons for limiting the tort to the sporting context for now.

First, the high visibility of racist conduct in sport arguably makes the behaviour more culpable, and thus deserving of a stronger legal response. Indeed, and as the FA Regulatory Commission outlined in *The Football Association v Suarez*, athletes are 'looked up to and admired' by many fans.[87] For instance, it was reported that a cumulative worldwide audience of 3.2 billion people tuned into the 2018/19 Premier League campaign.[88] In this light, Delgado's comments about the pervasive nature of racism may be rather instructive. In his words:

> Racism and racial stigmatization harm not only the victim and the perpetrator of individual racist acts but also society as a whole. Racism is a breach of the ideal of egalitarianism, that "all men are created equal" and each person is an equal moral agent, an ideal that is a cornerstone of… [our] moral and legal system… The failure of the legal system to redress the harms of racism, and of racial insults, conveys to all the lesson that egalitarianism is not a fundamental principle; the law, through inaction, implicitly teaches that respect for individuals is of little importance. Moreover, unredressed breaches of the egalitarian ideal may demoralize all those who prefer to live in a truly equal society, making them unwilling participants in the perpetuation of racism and racial inequality.[89]

In other words, racism does not just affect those on the receiving end of an insult – it also victimises society as a whole. This is, of course, magnified when the racist behaviour occurs in front of millions of onlookers and is distributed on various forms of media across the globe, as is often the case in professional sport. As Bleich explains, public acts of racism can reinforce 'negative stereotypes that contribute to ongoing discrimination against vulnerable groups'.[90] Seen in this way, it may not strictly be true that limiting a new tort of hate speech to the sporting context only provides a remedy to privileged athletes and not to other members of disadvantaged groups. By clamping down on discriminatory remarks made in such a highly visible setting by individuals who are often (and perhaps erroneously[91]) held up as role models, this may send out a symbolic message to the millions of onlookers that discriminatory abuse ought to be denounced and eradicated. In turn, this may provide greater protection to those in society who are most likely to be subjected to racial abuse.

The second reason for limiting the scope of a new tort of hate speech to sport is an altogether more practical one. As mentioned, whilst I would not object to this tort applying to all racist remarks in every setting, it is arguable that a sport-specific tort of hate speech is a more likely development in the current law. This is reflected in Bernstein's work, as she observes that the more conservative a recommendation is for a new tort, the more likely it is to succeed.[92] As she further elaborates, advocates of new torts are much more likely to be successful if they subscribe to the school of thought known as formalism, which emphasises 'analogy, synthesis [and] small increments that move the law forward'.[93] A sport-specific tort of hate speech to regulate discriminatory on-the-field conduct is arguably a less radical development that keeps the tort within relatively narrow confines. A generally applicable tort of hate speech is a much bolder proposition, not least because it may lead to an abundance of civil law claims.[94] It is perhaps for such reasons that scholars who have recently proposed other new torts have similarly tried to narrow down the parameters of their suggested torts in order to 'avoid raising floodgates concerns'.[95] As such, if we are to maximise the chances of introducing a new tort of hate speech, it may be prudent to insistent on a limited application to certain specific contexts for the time being.

Conclusion

To a certain extent, the law may 'only ever be a blunt instrument for eradicating racism' in sport.[96] More stringent regulatory measures by governing bodies – such as, for instance, lengthy bans and docking points – might prove to be a more effective long-term measure to combat discrimination in sport. However, as this chapter has argued, it may be necessary to supplement these regulatory provisions with an effective legal response too. This is perhaps best evidenced by CRT, which highlights that the imposition of vicarious liability may be necessary if we wish to expose the systemic racism that continues to plague many professional sports clubs. Although some may question whether non-legal theories such as CRT are relevant to this debate, I have argued for an interdisciplinary, legal realist conception of vicarious liability that is sensitive to insights from a wide array of disciplines. This is likely to lead to two immediate benefits.

First, it may help to produce better results in practice by enriching the more traditional rationales for vicarious liability. Indeed, if a certain theory or concept is relevant, it would be remiss to ignore it simply because it is not a 'legal' source. Second, the consideration of interdisciplinary theories such as CRT may be useful when applying the close connection test in this context. After all, if it can be established that a club is institutionally racist, this makes it much more difficult for the club to deny responsibility for on-the-field racism by arguing that their player was acting on a frolic of their own.

Whilst we see in other chapters that vicarious liability may be able to adequately respond to on-the-field personal injuries (Chapter 2) or even off-the-field sexual abuse (Chapters 4 and 5), this chapter argues that it is far more difficult to establish the responsibility of an employer for on-the-field discrimination. This was evidenced by looking at the following three causes of action: vicarious liability for a common law tort; statutory vicarious liability under the EA 2010; and vicarious liability for breach of a statutory duty under the PHA 1997. After recognising various limitations in these three options, this chapter argues that we ought to introduce a new tort of hate speech. The wrong at the core of this tort should be based in discrimination (rather than harassment), and it could be used to hold a club vicariously liable for on-the-field racist abuse. Finally, the high visibility of this discriminatory behaviour – allied to the practical limitations of introducing a more generally applicable tort of hate speech – may justify, at least for now, limiting this new tort specifically to the (professional) sporting context.

Notes

1 See, e.g., Paul MacInnes, 'Morecambe's Yann Songo'o Gets Six-Game Ban for Homophobic Slur' (*The Guardian*, 18 March 2021) <https://www.theguardian.com/football/2021/mar/18/morecambe-yann-songoo-gets-six-game-ban-for-homophobic-slur>.
2 Home Office, 'Football-Related Arrests and Banning Orders, England and Wales: 2021 to 2022 Season' (*Home Office*, 22 September 2022), <https://www.gov.uk/government/statistics/football-related-arrests-and-banning-orders-england-and-wales-2021-to-2022-season/football-related-arrests-and-banning-orders-england-and-wales-2021-to-2022-season> (noting that hate crime incidents were reported at 384 matches).
3 ibid.
4 Phoebe Williams, 'Performing in a Racially Hostile Environment' (1996) 6 Marq Sports LJ 287, 314.
5 Jamie Cleland and Ellis Cashmore, 'Fans, Racism and British Football in the Twenty-First Century: The Existence of a "Colour-Blind" Ideology' (2014) 40 J Ethn Migr Stud 638, 640.
6 See Stefan Lawrence and Christian Davis, 'Fans for Diversity? A Critical Race Theory Analysis of Black, Asian and Minority Ethnic (BAME) Supporters' Experiences of Football Fandom' (2019) 11 Int J Sport Policy Politics 701, 703.
7 *The Football Association v Suarez*, FA Regulatory Commission 20 December 2011.
8 *The Football Association v Terry*, FA Regulatory Commission 24–27 September 2012. Terry was not, however, convicted of any criminal offence. His defence was that he used the heinous phrase merely to repeat what he assumed Ferdinand had accused him of saying. See *R v Terry* (unreported), Westminster Magistrates' Court, 13 July 2012.
9 BBC, 'Welsh Club Player Banned for Eight Weeks for Racist Comments' (*BBC News*, 28 February 2020) <https://www.bbc.co.uk/sport/rugby-union/51679677>.
10 Associated Press, 'PK Subban 'Embarrassed' for Ice Hockey after Alleged Racist Abuse of Brother' (*The Guardian*, 24 January 2022) <https://www.theguardian.com/sport/2022/jan/24/pk-subban-jordan-subban-jacob-panetta-racism-allegations-hockey>.
11 Nick Hoult, 'Ashar Zaidi Calls for Crackdown on Racist Chants after Craig Overton Ban' (*The Telegraph*, 13 December 2015) <https://www.telegraph.co.uk/sport/cricket/counties/12048520/Ashar-Zaidi-calls-for-crackdown-on-racist-rants-after-Craig-Overton-ban.html>.

12 Australian Associated Press, 'Dogs' Sherman Suspended for Racial Slur' (*ABC News*, 27 June 2011) <https://www.abc.net.au/news/2011-06-27/dogs-sherman-suspended-for-racial-slur/2773462>.

13 Epifanio San Juan Jr., 'From Race to Class Struggle: Re-Problematizing Critical Race Theory' (2005) 11 Mich J Race & L 75, 79–80.

14 Brian Tamanaha, *Beyond the Formalist-Realist Divide: The Role of Politics in Judging* (Princeton University Press 2010) 1. See also Duncan Kennedy, 'Form and Substance in Private Law Adjudication' (1976) 89 Harv L Rev 1685.

15 Allan Hutchinson and Patrick Monahan, 'Law, Politics, and the Critical Legal Scholars' (1984) 36 Stan L Rev 199, 199.

16 Gloria Ladson-Billings, 'Just What is Critical Race Theory and What's it Doing in A Nice Field Like Education?' (1998) 11 Int J Qual Stud Educ 7, 11.

17 Kevin Hylton, *'Race' and Sport: Critical Race Theory* (Routledge 2009) 22.

18 ibid.

19 San Juan Jr (n 13) 79–80.

20 Richard Polenberg, *The World of Benjamin Cardozo: Personal Values and the Judicial Process* (HUP 1997) 162–3.

21 Derrick Bell, 'Racial Realism' (1992) 24 Conn L Rev 363, 363–4; Emily Houh, 'Critical Race Realism: Re-Claiming the Antidiscrimination Principle Through the Doctrine of Good Faith in Contract Law' (2005) 66 U Pitt L Rev 455, 457.

22 Roscoe Pound, 'The Scope and Purpose of Sociological Jurisprudence' (1911) 25 Harv L Rev 489, 512–3.

23 See, e.g., Rick Glofcheski, 'A Frolic in the Law of Tort: Expanding the Scope of Employers' Vicarious Liability' (2004) 12 Tort L Rev 18, 38–9; Lewis Klar, 'Judicial Activism in Private Law' (2001) 80 Can Bar Rev 215, 240.

24 Dan Priel, 'Two Forms of Formalism' in Andrew Robertson and James Goudkamp (eds), *Form and Substance in the Law of Obligations* (Hart 2019) 182–3.

25 ibid 180.

26 Yuval Noah Harari, *Sapiens: A Brief History of Humankind* (Harper 2015) 114–24.

27 Hanoch Dagan, 'The Realist Conception of Law' (2007) 57 UTLJ 607, 610.

28 ibid.

29 Hanoch Dagan, *Reconstructing American Legal Realism and Rethinking Private Law Theory* (OUP 2013) 61.

30 Karl Llewellyn, *The Common Law Tradition* (Little Brown & Co 1960) 36–8.

31 Richard Delgado and Jean Stefancic, *Critical Race Theory: An Introduction* (NYU Press 2012) xvii.

32 Martha Chamallas, 'Vicarious Liability in Torts: The Sex Exception' (2013) 48 Val UL Rev 133, 172.

33 Margaret Hall, 'After Waterhouse: Vicarious Liability and the Tort of Institutional Abuse' (2000) 22 J Soc Welf Fam Law 159, 162.

34 Sean Ingle, 'English Cricket is "Racist, Sexist and Elitist", Says Landmark Report' (*The Guardian*, 27 June 2023) <https://www.theguardian.com/sport/2023/jun/27/english-cricket-is-racist-sexist-and-elitist-says-landmark-report>.

35 Independent Commission for Equity in Cricket, 'Holding Up a Mirror to Cricket' (*ICEC*, 26 June 2023), <https://theicec.com/report/> 10.

36 ibid 112.

37 ibid 171.

38 Murad Ahmed, 'The Whiteness of English Cricket Breeds Racism' (*Financial Times*, 05 November 2021) <https://www.ft.com/content/0af5fe21-5ee1-46fb-8c1b-a27dbf008cb3> (referring to the 'systematic taunting' of Muslim players at YCCC).

39 Martyn Herman and Rohith Nair, 'English Cricket Rife with Racism, My Life Made "Hell" Says Rafiq' (*Reuters*, 17 November 2021) <https://www.reuters.com/lifestyle/sports/asian-heritage-cricketers-insulted-humiliated-yorkshire-rafiq-says-2021-11-16/>.

40 Manish Pandey, 'Azeem Rafiq: "Racist Language Isn't Friendly Banter," say British-Pakistanis' (*BBC News*, 05 November 2021) <https://www.bbc.co.uk/news/newsbeat-59081887>.

41 Tim Baker, 'Yorkshire Cricket Racism: From Azeem Rafiq to Alex Hales, the Key People Involved in the Storm – and What They Have Said' (*Sky News*, 06 December 2021) <https://news.sky.com/story/from-rafiq-to-vaughan-the-key-people-involved-in-the-racism-storm-engulfing-cricket-and-what-they-have-said-12460603>.

42 ICEC (n 35) 85.

43 BBC, 'Collingwood: Australian Football League Club "Guilty of Systemic Racism"' (*BBC News*, 01 February 2021) <https://www.bbc.co.uk/news/world-australia-55882443>.

44 Daniel Burdsey, *Racism in English Football: For Club and Country* (Routledge 2021).

45 Daniel Burdsey, 'They Think It's All Over… it Isn't Yet! The Persistence of Structural Racism and Racialised Exclusion in Twenty-First Century Football' in Daniel Burdsey (ed), *Race, Ethnicity and Football: Persisting Debates and Emergent Issues* (Routledge 2011) 7.

46 Joseph Kenney, 'Showing On-Field Racism the Red Card: How the Use of Tort Law and Vicarious Liability can Save the MLS from Joining the English Premier League on Racism Row' (2013) 20 Jeffrey S. Moorad Sports LJ 247, 291.

47 For example, s.5 of the Public Order Act 1986 makes it a criminal offence to use threatening or abusive words or behaviour within the hearing or sight of a person if this is likely to cause harassment, alarm or distress. An aggravated version of this offence is contained in s.4A and covers cases where the defendant intends to cause harassment, alarm or distress.

48 The facts of *Wilkinson v Downton* [1897] 2 QB 57 concerned a defendant who concocted a false story about injuries to the claimant's husband as a practical joke.

49 [2016] AC 219, [73] (Baroness Hale and Lord Toulson).

50 See, e.g., Alastair Gillespie, 'Racism in Cricket – Whose Liability?' (2022) 172 NLJ 15.

51 [2016] UKSC 11.

52 Unreported, IT Case No 2102426\97.

53 Notably, this case was dealt with under the Race Relations Act 1976. This Act, as well as other existing equality legislation, was consolidated under the EA 2010.

54 For confirmation of this point, see *Unite the Union v Nailard* [2018] EWCA Civ 1203. Until 2013, an employer was also responsible, under s.40 of the EA 2010, for harassment committed by third parties against their employees. Although this provision was later repealed, the UK government have recently committed to (re) introducing protection against third party harassment. See Government Equalities Office, 'Government Response to Consultation on Sexual Harassment in the Workplace' (Government Equalities Office, 21 July 2021) <https://www.gov.uk/government/consultations/consultation-on-sexual-harassment-in-the-workplace>.

55 Note also the incident involving Miami Dolphins lineman Jonathan Martin, who routinely referred to his teammate Richie Incognito as a 'nigger'. See Matthew Mitten et al., *Sports Law and Regulation: Cases, Materials, and Problems* (5th edn, Wolters Kluwer Law & Business 2019) 758.

56 As noted by Simon Gardiner et al., *Sports Law* (4th edn, Routledge 2012) 478, the 'most likely context in professional sport in which black players will be subject to racist abuse is on the field of play by members of the opposing team'.

57 The master's tort theory is encapsulated in the Latin maxim *qui facit per alium facit per se* ('he who acts through another does the act himself').

58 Paula Giliker, *Vicarious Liability in Tort: A Comparative Perspective* (CUP 2010) 15–6; Claire McIvor, *Third Party Liability in Tort* (Hart 2006) 4. As we saw in the

previous chapter, there may also be good practical reasons to keep a primary liability claim distinct from vicarious liability.

59 Employers seeking to rely upon s.109(4) are now required to regularly review their guidelines to ensure that their employees understand and comply with such equality policies. See, e.g., *Ms S Tesfagiorgis v Aspinalls Club Ltd, Mr M Branson, Ms L Attrill* (Case No. 2202256/2020), [315]-[21] (Elliott J).

60 Robert Stevens, 'Vicarious Liability or Vicarious Action?' (2007) 123 LQR 30, 32; *Staveley Iron & Chemical Co Ltd v Jones* [1956] AC 627, 639 (Lord Morton).

61 [2006] UKHL 34.

62 Patrick Atiyah, *Vicarious Liability in the Law of Torts* (Butterworths 1967) 280–4.

63 [2005] EWCA Civ 251, [38].

64 *Majrowski* (n 61), [16]–[7].

65 *Majrowski* (n 63), [56].

66 Simon Gardiner and Roger Welch, 'Football, Racism and The Limits Of 'Colour Blind' Law: Revisited' in Burdsey (n 45) 233.

67 Williams (n 4).

68 See, e.g., *Thomas v News Group Newspapers Ltd* [2001] EWCA Civ 1233, [30] (Lord Phillips).

69 *Majrowski* (n 61), [66].

70 ibid [30] (Lord Nicholls).

71 *Terry* (n 8). On the requirement for harassment to be serious enough to also sustain criminal liability, see *Conn v Council of City of Sunderland* [2008] IRLR 324.

72 As evidenced by *Kelly v DPP* [2003] Crim LR 43, 'separate' is perhaps a relative term here. In this case, leaving three messages on an answering machine was a course of conduct, despite the fact that all three messages were listened to on the same occasion.

73 Simon Gardiner, 'Disciplinary Provisions for Hate Speech in Football: Comparative Perspectives' (2015) 18 Sport Soc 552, 554.

74 [2003] UKHL 53, [46].

75 Gardiner and Welch (n 66) 233–4.

76 Lyn Tjon Soei Len and Anniek de Ruijter, 'Conceptualising the Tortuous Harms of Sexist and Racist Hate Speech' (2023) 2 ELO 8, 11.

77 Richard Delgado, 'Words that Wound: A Tort Action for Racial Insults, Epithets, and Name-Calling' (1982) 17 Harv CR-CLL Rev 133, 179.

78 ibid 181.

79 See, e.g., HL Deb 24 January 1997, Vol 1, col 917.

80 See, e.g., Sandra Fredman, 'Equality: A New Generation?' (2001) 30 ILJ 145.

81 Hugh Collins, 'Discrimination, Equality and Social Inclusion' (2003) 66 MLR 16.

82 Simon Gardiner and Louisa Riches, 'Racism and Homophobia in English Football: The Equality Act, Positive Action and the Limits of Law' (2016) 16 Int J Discrim Law 102, 105.

83 Cass Sunstein, 'On the Expressive Function of Law' (1996) 144 U Pa L Rev 2021, 2027–8.

84 [1997] 2 All ER 395, [43].

85 ibid [42].

86 [2023] UKSC 15, [58].

87 *Suarez* (n 7), [441].

88 Premier League, 'Premier League Global Audience on the Rise' (*Premier League*, 16 July 2019) <https://www.premierleague.com/news/1280062>.

89 Delgado (n 77) 140–1.

90 Erik Bleich, *The Freedom to be Racist?* (OUP 2011) 148.

91 The role model status of professional athletes in considered in more detail in Chapter 5.

92 Anita Bernstein, 'How to Make a New Tort: Three Paradoxes' (1997) 75 Tex L Rev 1539, 1543.
93 ibid 1545. In this light, it may be arguable that a new tort to capture racist slurs has a greater chance of being created if it operates as a slight modification to the law on harassment (rather than being predicated on anti-discrimination). However, as I argue above, there are good reasons to believe that a new civil wrong to target racial slurs would be able to better achieve the political ambitions of CRT if it is aligned with the anti-discrimination policy of egalitarianism.
94 This was a concern raised, and ultimately rejected, by Delgado (n 77) 171–2.
95 See, e.g., Andrea Mulligan, 'A Vindicatory Approach to Tortious Liability for Mistakes in Assisted Human Reproduction' (2020) 40 LS 55, 72 (proposing a new tort of 'interference with reproductive endeavours' instead of the wider tort of 'interference with reproductive autonomy').
96 Gardiner and Welch (n 66) 234.

4 Vicarious Liability for Off-the-Field Acts

A Risk-Based Approach to Hazing and Sexual Assault

Introduction

In March 2016, footballer Adam Johnson was sentenced to six years' imprisonment after pleading guilty to sexual activity with a child contrary to s.9 of the Sexual Offences Act 2003. It was held that the athlete had digitally penetrated a 15-year old girl in an act which the lead prosecutor described as a 'calculated, considered and carefully orchestrated' exploitation of his celebrity status.[1] The besotted victim was an avid fan of both Johnson and his employing club, Sunderland AFC, and it was reported that she would often wait outside the club's stadium in an attempt to catch a glimpse of her 'idol'.[2] As part of his grooming process (which also violated s.15 of the Act), Johnson offered the girl a signed Sunderland shirt in return for a 'thank you kiss',[3] an act which the presiding judge described as a clear 'abuse of trust' of the position in which the defendant, a revered elite footballer, had been placed.[4]

Although it was reported that the victim 'never sought financial gain' for this harm,[5] it is interesting to consider whether Johnson's employer might have been held vicariously liable had the young girl also pursued damages in a civil suit. This is becoming an increasingly pertinent issue in light of the multitude of news stories outlining similar allegations against other professional athletes.[6] Consequently, and in contrast to the previous chapters, the discussion here grapples with the question of whether sports clubs should be held vicariously liable for the *off*-the-field conduct of their athletes.

Two brief introductory points ought to be made here. First, whilst it is recognised that sports stars commit a variety of offences away from the field (ranging, for instance, from drink driving to fighting in nightclubs), there is a heavy emphasis on sexual harm in this chapter. As illustrated by the so-called 'Summer of Hell' in the National Rugby League ('NRL') in Australia, off-the-field gendered violence by professional athletes is currently a significant issue for many sports clubs. During the 2018 off-season, there was a 'string of high-profile [NRL] players accused of serious acts of violence and misconduct against women', with athletes implicated in a different off-the-field scandal once every 22 days.[7] This focus on sexual abuse also

DOI: 10.4324/9781032665870-4

allows me to illustrate how insights from the interdisciplinary field of gender studies might be applied to help determine the appropriate scope of vicarious liability in this context. Second, it is worth briefly clarifying here why a claim against an athlete's employer may be necessary at all. After all, if Johnson's victim did wish to pursue a civil claim for damages, surely it would be easier (and more logical) for her to commence a direct claim against the pecunious perpetrator himself? Two reasons, however, lead me to doubt whether this suggestion is entirely correct.

First, it should be noted that not all athletes are as well remunerated as Johnson was. For lower league footballers who are convicted of sexual assault – such as Ched Evans during his stint in League 1 with Sheffield United,[8] and Tyrell Robinson at League 2's Bradford City[9] – it may be necessary for claimants to seek recourse to the deeper pockets of the tortfeasor's employer. This may also be the case in sports that continue to impose salary caps, such as rugby union and basketball.

Second, even if a professional athlete *was* the recipient of a handsome salary during their playing career, it must be recognised that a conviction for a serious off-the-field offence is likely to effectively end the wrongdoer's career, as it did with Johnson.[10] In this regard, there is no guarantee that an athlete will be able to fully afford a significant damages award (which will often be imposed many years after the incident), particularly if they were unable to work during that time. This is also reinforced by the vast judicial discretion evident under s.33 of the Limitation Act 1980 to circumvent the traditional three-year period in which to commence a civil claim.[11] Given the startlingly high levels of bankruptcy amongst retired professional athletes,[12] it may well be necessary for a victim to also sue the tortfeasor's former employer when pursuing a claim in which the limitation period has been disapplied.

With these points in mind, I attempt to clarify the contours of my risk-based approach in this context by highlighting several introductory points. In particular, I suggest that the theory of risk is a suitable indicator of vicarious liability for off-the-field harm, especially as cases in other closely related areas of law – such as privacy and unfair dismissal – also appear to adopt risk-based methodology when assessing the extramural activity of individuals. Furthermore, and in recognising that the analysis in this chapter ought to be confined solely to the *professional* sporting context, I further highlight the need for an empirical and interdisciplinary approach to vicarious liability, and this is best evidenced by illustrating the importance of gender studies to this particular area of law. When off-the-field sexual harm is viewed through this critical lens, it is revealed that both the hazing of young athletes and the sexual abuse of women away from the sports field could lead to the vicarious liability of professional sports clubs.

Accordingly, this chapter utilises the concept of masculinities studies to consider the scope of vicarious liability for sexual abuse committed during hazing and initiation rituals. It critically examines *GB v Stoke City Football*

Club Ltd,[13] which is currently the only case to examine the vicarious liability of a professional sports club for the off-the-field conduct of an athlete. The chapter argues that a more normatively desirable outcome could have been reached in that case had the judge engaged more thoroughly with masculinities studies as part of a risk-based analysis. Notably, empirical data appears to support the view that vicarious liability ought to be imposed for such conduct, although it is ultimately recognised that more UK-based research may be required in order to corroborate this finding.

Finally, I argue that professional sports clubs could also be held vicariously liable for one of their athletes sexually assaulting a woman. This is illustrated with reference to feminist legal theory, which highlights that the toxic and misogynistic culture of many sports operates as a key risk factor for off-the-field sexual abuse. This is also reinforced by the belief held by some athletes that they are entitled to easy sexual access to women's bodies simply because they are successful sportsmen. The chapter concludes by highlighting that such harm is not merely coincidental, and that these risk factors could support the claim that one's employment as a professional athlete makes a material contribution to the off-field sexual harm suffered by their victims.

Clarifying the Contours of the Risk-Based Analysis: Four Introductory Points

In contrast to most other decisions on vicarious liability, it must be recognised that the typical employee in our off-the-field sports context is a rather unique tortfeasor. Unlike in those cases involving well-known national juggernauts such as Morrisons and Barclays Bank, the wrongdoer in the current context is an esteemed professional athlete who, in some instances, might even be more popular and influential than their own employer.[14] Particularly since the turn of the twenty-first century, Whannel notes that there has been 'an erosion of a clear distinction between public and private domains' for elite athletes,[15] which may simply be just another way of saying that the line between 'on-duty' and 'off-duty' has been significantly blurred for these celebrity employees.

This development was likely spurred by both advancements in technology and the broader commercialisation and commodification of professional sport,[16] with fans arguably being just as concerned (if not *more* concerned) with the off-field exploits of their favourite players as they are with their on-pitch achievements.[17] As testament to this fact, many sports stars are showered with a plethora of sponsors, and various scholars have even suggested that some athletes (and particularly those competing in the upper echelons of their sport) can be viewed as brands in their own right.[18] As the famous basketball player LeBron James has recently attested to, the culture of celebrity that is now prevalent in much of modern society has meant that 'the first time [he] stepped on an NBA court, [he] became a businessman'.[19]

With this in mind, it is perhaps worth making four introductory points about the contours of my risk-based analysis for off-the-field sexual harm. First, it is clear that the blurred line between 'on-duty' and 'off-duty' conduct only really applies to professional sport. Amateur athletes are not celebrities, and there is no sense in which we can state that they are still 'on-duty' for their club when conducting themselves away from the pitch. As such, whilst the discussion of vicarious liability for on-the-field acts in the previous two chapters could perhaps apply to both the amateur and semi-professional context, it must be noted that my risk-based analysis of off-the-field conduct in this (and the following) chapter is only applicable to the professional sports industry. This is not to say, however, that the analysis in these chapters is limited specifically to this context. It could, for instance, prove of wider interest to those concerned with employer liability for other famous tortfeasors, particularly those involved in the entertainment industry. After all, it has yet to be tested, in either the literature or case law, whether the unique factual matrix provided by one's celebrity status can (or indeed should) influence the scope of the close connection test.

Second, the focus in this chapter on the inherent risks or characteristics of a particular sport can be justified in light of a similar methodology in other (closely related) areas of law. For instance, in relation to privacy, Nicol J in *Ferdinand v MGN* suggested that the decision to find in favour of Prince Caroline of Monaco in *Von Hannover v Germany* was because the intrusive photographs of the claimant in this case did not call into question 'her fitness to perform the ceremonial duties which her status required'.[20] Similar judicial sentiments were also expressed in *AMC v News Group Newspapers Ltd*, a case which concerned a married professional athlete attempting to block the publication of his affair with another woman. Here, Laing J observed that being a professional athlete did not make the claimant 'an example in every sphere of his existence'; importantly, '[a]ny scrutiny of [the claimant's] conduct away from sport ought to bear a reasonable relationship with the fact that he is a sportsman'.[21]

A similar enquiry is also utilised in unfair dismissal cases, with judges reiterating that 'a dismissal for misconduct outside the workplace can only be justified where there is sufficient connection between the crime committed and the employee's work'.[22] As such, dismissal for theft by a department store worker could be justified in light of the clear link between shoplifting and the employee's role,[23] but a barrister's disbarment for drink driving manslaughter would be unfair because it has 'neither connexion nor significance for any professional functions as a barrister'.[24] Notably, the claimant professional rugby player in *Mason v Huddersfield Giants Ltd* was held to have been unfairly dismissed, given the absence of an intrinsic link between his role as an athlete and his failure to promptly remove a picture of his teammate's anus on his personal Twitter page.[25]

Of course, by highlighting these examples, I do not mean to suggest that a case in one area of law should be strictly followed in another. The underlying policy basis of each area of law is different, so just because an athlete was justifiably dismissed for a certain action does not necessarily mean that this also gives rise to a sufficient nexus to hold the employer strictly liable (and vice versa). Sanders has illustrated this point in some detail when she highlighted, based on comments in *Lister v Hesley Hall Ltd*,[26] that a school would not be vicariously liable for sexual abuse committed by a groundsman.[27] She contrasts this with *P v Nottinghamshire County Council*,[28] a case in which the dismissal of a school groundsman for a sexual offence against his own daughter at home was justified, because of the potential risk of him committing a similar act on children in the school. Consequently, whilst the two tests do appear to sometimes point in different directions,[29] it must be recognised that the necessity of establishing an intrinsic connection between an enterprise and a particular risk is a common trend throughout other areas of law that seek to regulate the extramural activities of individuals. This arguably provides a further justification for adopting a risk-based approach to the close connection test in this context.

The third point of clarification is that, when considering the connection between a sport and the relevant off-the-field risk, we ought to assess whether any conclusion could be empirically justified. The importance of adopting an empirical enquiry for the purposes of vicarious liability was discussed in Chapter 2, and this argument will be further developed here. In particular, the adoption of an empirical approach will require me to draw upon observations from some interdisciplinary fields, most notably gender studies. This area of research comprises several relevant frameworks, two of which are considered especially useful for our purposes: masculinity studies and feminist theory. To a large extent, both of these perspectives overlap, and it is unsurprising that Kimmel has referred to masculinity studies as a 'significant outgrowth of feminist studies and an ally to its older sister in a complex and constantly shifting relationship'.[30] As such, whilst both subfields are clearly relevant to the overarching issue of gendered violence, masculinity studies – which centres on the 'damaging impact of patriarchy on men'[31] – will be geared more towards harm suffered by male athletes in sport. In contrast, the lens of feminist theory is reserved more for violence perpetrated by professional sportsmen against women.

In adopting this approach, the discussion in this chapter may be of both narrow and broad appeal. It is narrow in the sense that it may reinforce, once again, how many of the traditional rationales for vicarious liability can be intellectually enhanced by a socio-legal, interdisciplinary approach. Its wider appeal lies in its potential contribution to the growing literature on feminist legal theory, particularly as it highlights tort law's broader failure to recognise appropriate remedies for gendered harms.

Furthermore, the focus on empirical study and feminist jurisprudence in this chapter is broadly consistent with my support for legal realism outlined in previous chapters. In particular, Quinn observes that the work of contemporary feminist legal scholars is 'seen as a direct descendant of the traditional antiformalist tale'.[32] It is noteworthy that some scholars have proclaimed Critical Legal Studies to be the progeny of legal realism,[33] as they both share the view that 'law is not systematically intelligible in its own terms'.[34] In this regard, Quinn has accurately posited that 'it is out of the rib of Critical Legal Studies that modern feminist jurisprudence is said to be born'.[35] She goes on to note that many scholars who subscribe to feminist legal theory have 'accepted the traditional framing of the running realist narrative',[36] and it is arguably for such reasons that a feminist perspective is a particularly enlightening one for this book.

The fourth (and final) introductory point is that my risk-based analysis in this chapter appears to cast serious doubt on Morgan's description of the scope of vicarious liability in the off-field sports context. Under his interpretation of the current law, a club will not be liable for an athlete assaulting a member of the public in a nightclub, nor will they be responsible for a player raping an individual whom they have met outside of club activities.[37] The following analysis normatively challenges this overly narrow descriptive stance, and directs attention to the appropriate scope of vicarious liability in two particular off-the-field contexts: firstly, the abuse of young athletes during initiation rites; and secondly, the sexual assault of women.

Sexual Abuse of Rookie Athletes

The only vicarious liability decision to deal with the off-the-field conduct of a professional sportsman is *GB v Stoke City Football Club Ltd*, a case which concerned the alleged sexual practice of 'gloving' by Stoke City FC's first-team goalkeeper Peter Fox during the 1980s.[38] This involved the senior player applying an ointment to a glove, and digitally penetrating the claimant's anus. This act was supposedly administered as an informal punishment to the claimant who had made a number of mistakes in his role as an apprentice footballer at the club (such as providing lukewarm tea for the senior players, and making an erroneous line call during training).[39] Due to the considerable period of time between the alleged act and the trial, HHJ Butler concluded that the claimant had not successfully proven, on the balance of probabilities, that he had in fact been gloved.[40] Nevertheless, His Honour did go on to consider whether vicarious liability could have been imposed upon Stoke City had the allegations in this case been verified.

In HHJ Butler's view, even if the claimant had been able to adduce sufficient evidence, the club would *not* have been held vicariously liable for this act, because they did not confer any express or implied power upon the tortfeasor to discipline youth players.[41] In Morgan's words, this creates an authority-based approach, with vicarious liability only being imposed where the tortfeasor exercises authority over the victim.[42] However, it is interesting that throughout this obiter section in *GB*, HHJ Butler drew upon two passages from prior cases which emphasised the importance of enterprise risk to the determination of vicarious liability.[43] Yet, on the facts of the immediate case, His Honour rejected an application of such a risk-based approach on the spurious grounds that it 'would involve an extension of the boundaries of vicarious liability beyond the parameters of the decided authorities'.[44]

GB, it is suggested, provides a fine example of how judicial reasoning could have been improved by the adoption of a more theoretical, interdisciplinary approach. Perhaps if counsel for the claimant had delivered a more theory-heavy pleading that challenged some of the defendants' more doubtful claims – such as the assertion that the sporting enterprise 'did not create or enhance the risk of that kind of behaviour occurring' to an apprentice[45] – then the judge may not have been able to skirt around this argument quite as easily.

Such a risk-based claim could have been predicated on the disparate power relations inherent in professional football. Notions of power and authority seemed to be at the heart of the 'conferral of authority' test that was applied by Males LJ in the Court of Appeal in *The Trustees of the Barry Congregation of Jehovah's Witnesses v BXB*.[46] However, this test – which informed the so-called 'tailored' approach to vicarious liability in cases involving sexual abuse – was ultimately rejected by the Supreme Court in *BXB*. Lord Burrows argued that the 'necessary tailoring' was already reflected in the close connection test,[47] and in his view, there was no need to consider whether an employer had conferred any authority on a wrongdoer. Whilst his Lordship may have been correct to move away from the concept of a 'tailored' test for sexual abuse, it is far more problematic, from a risk-based point of view, to fail to assess the power and authority enjoyed by a tortfeasor. Indeed, power and authority are surely relevant considerations when assessing the degree of risk that is intrinsic to a particular enterprise. As Chamberlain J opined at first instance in *BXB*, 'any organisation that confers on its leaders power and authority over others creates a risk that those leaders will abuse that power and authority'.[48]

As such, perhaps the relevant question that needs to be asked in determining whether a close connection existed in *GB* is whether Fox's status as an established first-team goalkeeper placed him in a position of power or authority over the apprentice footballers. HHJ Butler in *GB* appeared to think that it did not, as he was seemingly persuaded by the defendant's argument that even though the youngsters looked up to the senior players as role models, this 'did not amount to the conferring of a power over them'.[49]

This, I suggest, may be a rather erroneous conclusion. As was made clear by Chamberlain J in *BXB*, any organisation that 'sets its leaders up as moral...

exemplars... imbues those leaders with power and authority'.[50] As we will see in the following chapter, athletes may, on the basis of the wide-ranging disrepute clauses that are incorporated into their professional contracts, be held out as 'moral exemplars' by their own employers. Of course, the power exhibited by Fox in *GB* may not have been akin to the considerable power wielded by the tortfeasors in those cases involving priests[51] or police officers,[52] but it was still a significant degree of power given that the tortfeasor occupied a position in the first-team that young athletes sought to emulate. As such, it is worth remembering, as McLachlin J did in *Jacobi v Griffiths*, that 'power must be understood in context'.[53]

A further concern that was raised by HHJ Butler in *GB* was the potential ramifications of imposing vicarious liability on Stoke City. His Honour suggested that a finding of liability here would lead to all employers in every sector being held vicariously liable for any harm committed against an apprentice by a full-time employee.[54] This, it is argued, is a rather gross overgeneralisation that could have been avoided by a more explicit application of enterprise risk in this case. Indeed, just as the same act of sexual abuse by a groundsman in *Lister* would not have given risen to vicarious liability, it is not possible to say that assaulting a trainee in every other profession is just as likely to give rise to employer liability. The power disparity (and risk of abuse of such power) between, say, an apprentice and senior worker in the IT or retail industry is clearly different to that exhibited between a rookie and professional athlete in a physically invasive sport.

This is arguably reinforced by the necessarily young age of a rookie athlete (as opposed to a trainee in the banking or construction sector, for instance, who could plausibly be an adult). Whilst the Court of Appeal in *BXB* did not seek to distinguish between adult and child sexual abuse in their application of the 'tailored' approach in that case, it was recognised that it will generally be more difficult to establish a significant power disparity when the tortfeasor and victim are both adults.[55] This only serves to reinforce the contention that the power gap between an apprentice and full-time employee will not always be the same in every industry, and that a truly contextual approach is needed in this area of law.

The Relevance of Masculinities Studies

It was argued in the previous section that the risk of abuse of power is inherent in professional sport, and that such a power disparity could be used to inform a risk-based approach to vicarious liability for off-the-field sexual harm between teammates. This section aims to reinforce that contention with reference to masculinities studies, which may help to demonstrate that the risk of sexual harm is far more intrinsic to elite sport than it is to most other industries.

As previously touched upon, masculinities studies examines the notion of what it means to 'be a man', and in particular how the hegemonic masculinity prevalent in various cultures and institutions leads to the formation of socially dominant male groups. Consequently, it seems a particularly apt theory to apply here, especially as the overwhelming scholarly consensus appears to view professional sport as an 'active engine in the creation and preservation of power relationships'.[56] In fact, participation in sport is widely perceived to act as a 'masculinising process',[57] in that the emergence of modern sport in the late nineteenth century was reportedly a reaction to the concern that boys were becoming more feminine as a result of industrialisation.[58] This led to the embodiment of various militaristic characteristics in sport (such as an emphasis on aggression, discipline, toughness and obedience), and ultimately to a culture whereby individuals view 'other peoples' bodies as objects of their power and domination'.[59] As Brake observes, so long as athletes exhibit these traits, they are 'clothed with an enviable masculinity'.[60] With this in mind, three particular points are relevant here.

First, being 'masculine' is not to be strictly associated with being male. Masculinity is a cultural construction that is divorced from biology, so it may be that much of the discussion in this section is equally applicable to female athletes who embody hypermasculine traits in the locker room. Second, off-the-field sexual violence may only be an expected cultural norm in those sports that are described by scholars as 'quintessentially' masculine, such as rugby and football.[61] The practical significance of this is considered in the following chapter when I set out some useful guidelines for determining an employer's vicarious liability for off-the-field acts.

Finally, it is worth noting that, because masculinity is a socially constructed phenomenon, it must constantly be re-proven and reinforced, lest it be lost.[62] This produces a hierarchy of masculinities in the sports dressing room, with all athletes seeking to establish and reaffirm their position as the most dominant 'alpha-male' athlete.[63] As evidenced by the tortfeasor's actions in *GB*, one way to reach the apex of masculinity is to perpetrate violence against rookie athletes or those other male participants who do not easily fit into society's dominant conception of 'manliness'.[64] This violence is often sexual in nature, as Belkin notes that '[i]n almost every cultural and institutional context imaginable, penetration is associated with masculinity and dominance whilst penetrability is a marker of subordination'.[65] In this light, Adams, Anderson and McCormack argue that athletes 'employ the processes of hegemonic oppression to construct socially esteemed identities (predicated on being heterosexual and masculine), in an effort to maintain or improve their position within the social stratification'.[66] On the flip side, the ability to endure such pain and 'take it like a man' is also one way for young athletes to ascend the masculinity hierarchy,[67] particularly in light of the established cultural norm that, if they survive the ordeal, they might have the opportunity to exert their own power and dominance over an apprentice later in their career.

As we see from this discussion, it is suggested that exposure to masculinities studies may have aided HHJ Butler in understanding that Fox's behaviour in *GB* was, in fact, an expected and inherent risk of professional football, such that the vicarious liability of Stoke City should have been triggered had the events in question been factually proven. This conclusion may also be consistent with the discussion on benefit enterprise liability in Chapter 5, particularly if we accept that producing a tough, aggressive player was to Stoke City's advantage.

Notably, whilst *GB* was concerned with informal punishment, vicarious liability ought to also arise for any harm that is caused during initiation rituals too, as such harm is seemingly grounded in the same toxic masculine hegemony as punishment. These rituals, which are often referred to in North America as 'hazing',[68] are defined by Thompson, Johnstone and Banks as 'activities whereby senior members put incoming athletes through challenges in order to assimilate them into the team culture'.[69] These challenges are often sexual in nature, and they allow those at the top of the power hierarchy to feminise and emasculate the newcomers whilst further solidifying the heteromasculine identities of those involved.[70] In this light, Volkwein-Caplan and Sankaran are correct to argue that sexual hazing is 'particularly likely to occur in tightly knit competitive male groups (e.g. military units, gangs, college fraternities, sport) that bind men emotionally to one another and contributes to their seeing sex relations from a position of power and status'.[71]

It is perhaps no coincidence, then, that in one of the more recent UK cases to consider vicarious liability in the military context, the facts revolved heavily around a second lieutenant attempting to prove his masculine value and bravery to his peers by engaging in a daring jump from a bridge. The captain in command had put 'immense' pressure on the claimant to jump in order to prove that he was as brave as the other men in the group, and it was for such reasons that the Court of Appeal found that the negligence of the captain was committed within the course of his employment.[72]

Empirical Statistics and Jurisdictional Sensitivity

Now, in light of my legal realist and law-in-action-based approach to vicarious liability, it is perhaps helpful to briefly examine whether empirical facts can vindicate the normative intuitions outlined in the previous section. The available data suggests that they might. Aside from anecdotal evidence from former athletes themselves,[73] various US-based studies have found that between 42% and 74% of college athletes have been the victim of hazing,[74] with Waldron concluding that over 50% of such athletes were subject to what she labels 'severe hazing' (which includes brandings, physical beatings and sexual assault).[75] Similar statistics are evident in other countries, with Favero et al. outlining that 47.1% of Portuguese university athletes experienced some form of sexual hazing.[76] Recent findings from Kerschner and Allan confirm that this is a risk increased by sport, as they reported that 40.9% of US college athletes experienced hazing, as opposed to 24.8% of non-athletes.[77] Qualitative research by other scholars suggests that the rate of hazing is linked to the perceived masculinity of each sport, such that athletes are more likely to experience hazing in 'competitive, team and contact sports than in less competitive, individual and non-contact sports'.[78]

At first glance, it may seem rather peculiar to rely on statistics that are gleaned predominantly from the US collegiate sport context, particularly when we consider the well-rehearsed differences between the so-called 'American model' and 'European model' of sport. However, beyond the obvious regulatory differences, there arguably exists a striking similarity in relation to the underlying financial and cultural ethos between US college sport and UK professional sport. After all, US college sport – which is regulated by the National Collegiate Athletic Association ('NCAA') – is a multi-billion dollar industry that is watched by millions of fans across the globe.[79] For context, it is reported that the University of Texas' football team hosts a crowd of around 90,000 people every week, and it is estimated that the team generates almost $100 million a year for the university.[80] These figures – which would not look out of place in the top-flight of English football – are bolstered by the fact that the University of Texas has even introduced its own television network to broadcast the teams' games.[81]

In this light, it is little surprise that many college athletes in the US are often treated as celebrities, much like professional sports stars in the UK. Indeed, Gerrie notes that, during the 2014–15 season, Duke University's star player, Jahlil Okafor, was worth around $2.6m due to his immense 'identity, celebrity and star status'.[82] NCAA athletes are also accustomed to training for multiple hours each day, and are often supplied with cutting-edge facilities, equipment and diet plans in order to maximise their potential.[83] Consequently, it is perhaps unsurprising that these high-profile US college athletes are sometimes held out as role models that are able to influence social change.[84]

What this picture arguably shows, then, is that US college athletes are seemingly subjected to the same influences and competitive environment as many professional sports stars in the UK. In this light – and bearing in mind the 'special affinity' that appears to exist between the UK and US in terms of 'popular culture and sport'[85] – it could be concluded that those studies on the risk of hazing in US college sport may be instructive (although certainly not determinative) for the UK professional sporting industry too. In the absence of any UK-based empirical research into this issue – which, it is suggested, may provide a fruitful topic for further research – statistics from US collegiate sport may provide some support for the normative arguments outlined in the previous section.

Sexual Assault of Women

Unfortunately, off-the-field sexual abuse by professional athletes is not just directed towards teammates in the locker room. Athletes also use violence against women to demonstrate their masculinity, a point which once again reinforces the overlap between the two related fields of gender studies perused in this chapter. Notably, both women inside and outside of sport are at risk of such harm. As examples of the former, one need only delve into the purported misogynistic culture of sports such as figure skating,[86] cycling,[87] cheerleading,[88] golf[89] and horse racing.[90] In fact, Haynes has also discussed several recent examples of women footballers who have been subjected to sexual abuse 'at the hands of a sporting regime that is steeped in patriarchy'.[91]

However, for purposes of brevity, and because the previous section has already touched upon harm caused to participants who are directly involved in the sporting milieu, this section focusses on the sexual assault of women who are not current or aspiring professional athletes. This discussion will hopefully lay to rest the lingering scholarly suspicion that there is some form of 'geographical component' to the close connection test, as suggested by Lunney, Nolan and Oliphant.[92] Indeed, an application of vicarious liability to the professional sports industry allows us to tease out the fact that it is the *risk* of harm that ought to be the crucial determinant of liability, and *not* the physical proximity between the tortious act and the employer's establishment.[93] Therefore, because many athletes are expected to travel as part of their employment, it is not logical to maintain that sexual assault in a hotel room after an away game is any less susceptible to vicarious liability than a similar act of abuse committed near their employer's base of operations.

There are, of course, countless high-profile examples of professional athletes engaging in such acts all over the globe. Footballers Cristiano Ronaldo and Neymar, as well as basketballer Kobe Bryant, have all been accused of raping women in hotel rooms, and there have been a string of similar incidents involving players competing in the National Football League (NFL).[94] Comparable stories can also be identified in other physically invasive team sports such as rugby league, as evidenced by the 2010 incident in which six Huddersfield Giants players were arrested on suspicion of raping a woman during a pre-season tour in Newcastle.[95] In assessing whether such acts could give rise to vicarious liability, the question here is whether the risk of sexual assault against women is significantly heightened by the culture of professional sport (or whether, as some scholars suggest, the correlation between the harm and the employment is overstated due to the increased public attention on sporting celebrities).[96] As illustrated above, a feminist lens – which illuminates the marginalisation of women in society – is applied here in light of both (i) the gendered and androcentric nature of elite sport, and (ii) the fact that off-the-field sexual harm committed by sports stars against non-athletes disproportionately affects women.

The Relevance of Feminist Legal Theory

It must be noted that a feminist perspective is certainly not a mainstream consideration for the law on vicarious liability. Aside from some sporadic scholarly exposition,[97] the only explicit mention of feminist theory in the context of vicarious liability comes from Justice Souter's judgment in the US case of *Faragher v City of Boca Raton*.[98] Here, the sexual harassment of a female lifeguard by her two supervisors gave rise to vicarious liability due to the 'fairness of requiring the employer to bear the burden of foreseeable social behaviour'.[99] In reaching this conclusion, Justice Souter drew upon the feminist work of Susan Estrich to illustrate the importance of job-created power.[100]

In this regard, and in light of the aforementioned 'tailored' approach to sexual abuse (which, as we saw, similarly took into account the conferral of power and authority on tortfeasors), it may be that feminist legal scholarship has already been implicitly influencing the scope of vicarious liability in recent cases. If this is true, it would be preferable for judges to follow in the footsteps of Justice Souter and candidly admit this fact. Not only may this help to enrich an interdisciplinary, theory-based application of vicarious liability, but it may also assist us in demonstrating that the sexual assault of women is, in fact, an increased risk of the professional sports industry.

Indeed, feminist scholars have long outlined several explanations as to why the sexual assault of women is a particularly likely occurrence in professional sport, and many of these reasons are neatly summarised by the comments of Garo Mardirossian (an attorney for a female victim who accused an NBA coach of sexual assault in a hotel room in 2014). In his view, '[a]ided by their fame, money and power, and motivated by a culture that tolerates misogynistic gender bias, too many men in professional basketball inappropriately abuse women'.[101] In this, the suggestion is that the subculture of elite male sport both devalues and denigrates women, with the misogynistic peer norms operating as 'a key risk factor for men's perpetration of sexual violence'.[102]

Many athletes are often institutionalised into believing that they must detach themselves from any form of femininity, and in so doing they become 'aggressive towards females in order to see themselves above feminine, or feminine traits'.[103] In fact, feminist literature highlights numerous examples of toxic locker-room language in a variety of sports, with statements of hostility towards women often closely intertwined with phallocentric discussion of women as sexual objects.[104] In addition, male athletes are also accustomed to using phrases such as 'pussy' or 'girl' in a derogatory manner against their own teammates.[105] Such talk is often utilised as a means of reaffirming men's superiority over women, and multiple scholars argue that these attitudes create a 'rape-prone' culture that 'promotes and encourages' the sexual control and domination of women.[106] This has led commentors such as Kidd to scathingly describe the sporting dressing room as a 'training ground for rape'.[107]

Importantly for the purposes of enterprise (and vicarious) liability, many feminist writers in this context emphasise the institutional and organisational conditions that lead to such misogyny, rather than examining the traits of a few individual 'bad apples' who commit sexual harm. Indeed, Anderson's work highlights that placing male athletes in gender-integrated sports – as opposed to all-male gender-segregated sports – may actually reduce the chances of individual participants committing violence against women.[108] By way of example, consider Fogel's recent report of a university hockey athlete who committed rape simply because he was afraid of saying 'no' to his teammates (and not because he had any 'biological drive or impulse to commit sexual assault').[109]

In addition, psychological research in the area of social norms theory illustrates that if one possesses a belief that their peers are accepting of sexual violence, then that individual is more likely to commit sexual assault.[110] It is perhaps unsurprising, then, that recent studies suggest that 45% of sexual assault allegations against college football players in the US involved more than one offender.[111] This ought to be contrasted with figures on multiple perpetrator rapes in the wider US population, where it is estimated that only around 10% of sexual assaults involved more than one assailant.[112]

One explanation for this discrepancy is the toxic rape culture that is prevalent in many sports. This has sometimes resulted in off-the-field competitions between athletes who vie for the most sexual encounters or 'notches on the bedpost'.[113] One of the more recent examples of this occurred in 2019 when cricketer Alex Hepburn was convicted of rape after partaking in a 'deep-seated and long-running' sexual conquest game 'between a number of professional sportsmen'.[114] In this regard, and because engagement in a sexual act is often couched in the language of 'scoring', sex often becomes a game in itself to many individuals (and like most games, there are winners and losers). For professional athletes who are usually required to possess a win-at-all-costs mentality, they may seek to turn a loss (i.e. the rejection of their sexual advancements) into a win (i.e. engagement in a sexual act), often through physical force and violence. This is perhaps faintly reinforced by the conservative understandings of sex that are symbolically at play in the basic rules of many sports. For instance, and as Dundes observes, the ultimate goal for American football players is to 'assert their masculinity by penetrating the endzones of their rivals'.[115]

Finally, the hypermasculine subculture of professional sport provides another relevant – though, as we discuss in the following chapter, not necessarily unique – factor which may further enhance the risk of off-the-field sexual assault against women: the belief amongst participants that, due to their celebrity status and athletic success, they are entitled to easy sexual access to women's bodies.[116] As the former NBA star Dennis Rodman once boasted, '[a]s long as I play ball, I can get any woman I want'.[117] This was seemingly a feature of Adam Johnson's criminal trial, in which the lead prosecutor suggested that it was 'an excessive arrogance and an unwarranted level of expectation' that brought Johnson to the courtroom.[118] Such feelings of entitlement have arguably been ingrained in sport for many decades, with the instigator of the modern Olympics, Pierre de Coubertin, even maintaining in 1912 that 'female applause' should be awarded for male athleticism.[119] Of course, if sex with a woman is suddenly unavailable, an athlete steeped in a culture of fame and expectation may feel entitled to seize what he believes he deserves.

These feelings of entitlement are also compounded by research that suggests that women are most attracted to men who play aggressive and competitive sports.[120] This may lead to professional athletes erroneously assuming that all women crave a sexual encounter with sports stars, thus marking all women as 'virtually unrapeable'.[121] As was demonstrated by the public reaction to the rape allegations made against Kobe Bryant,[122] athletes are oftentimes depicted as the target of promiscuous women, and such victim-blaming ideologies arguably only serve to reinforce the acceptability to athletes of sexually assaulting a woman who has been disparagingly referred to (by both peers and the media) as a 'gold-digger'.[123]

Further Considerations: Empirical Data and Methodological Issues

Taken together, the arguments in the previous section provide a solid foundation upon which to argue that off-the-field sexual assault of women is an intrinsic and heightened risk of professional sport, and therefore an act for which clubs could be held vicariously liable. Additionally, numerous statistics also demonstrate that it is empirically – and not just normatively – desirable to impose strict liability on sports clubs for such acts. Building upon the similar findings of earlier studies conducted in the 1990s,[124] Young et al. found that 54.3% of surveyed university athletes in the US engaged in some form of sexual assault against women, as opposed to 37.9% of non-athletes.[125] Other investigations portray a similar trend, with a 2019 study concluding that NCAA athletes were disciplined for sexual misconduct at a rate three times higher than the general student population.[126] Empirical research also suggests that athletes are more likely to accept 'rape myths' (distorted beliefs about rape that are used to justify sexual violence),[127] as well as being more confused about the appropriate boundaries of sexual consent.[128] This is perhaps an unsurprising by-product of their erroneous assumption that all women desire sexual intercourse with them. It is important to mention, however, two caveats on these empirical findings.

First, and as was touched upon earlier in this chapter, much of this data is limited to collegiate and university sport, and there has unfortunately been an alarming lack of research on the prevalence of off-the-field sexual assault amongst *professional* athletes. This is likely because, as McCray notes, the research on the relationship between sporting participation and violence against women has largely stagnated since the turn of the twenty-first century.[129]

Second, it may be that the current empirical data also conceals a rather important methodological issue. It has thus far been presumed that it is the toxic culture of sport that increases the risk of sexual violence against women. However, it might well be the case that certain personality types who are prone to such behaviour are simply attracted to these aggressive sports in the first place. To the extent that this is the case, it may not be appropriate to impose vicarious liability. This is because the employment context would not then be causally linked to the injury, but would rather only be setting the time and space for the wrong without necessarily increasing its likelihood. On this basis, the employer's involvement in the harm would simply be coincidental, and the law has already determined that no tortious liability should ensue for coincidental injury.[130]

The answer may not, however, be an either/or one. In fact, it seems plausible that *both* factors might be operating here to generate the increased risk of sexual assault. As Hall observes, '[t]here are, undoubtedly, stereotypical 'bees' drawn to residential 'honey pots' (bringing in sadistic/predatory norms); but it also appears likely that certain institutional conditions... tend to produce abusive behaviour in hitherto 'normal' adults'.[131] In order to find a close connection, then, Binnie J in *Jacobi* outlined that the employment must have 'materially' and 'significantly contributed to the occurrence of the harm'.[132] According to cases in the related area of causation, a 'material contribution' may simply be one that is more than *de minimis*.[133] This is largely in accordance with Sykes' law-and-economics analysis, in which he highlighted that even a 'partial cause' would still be enough to warrant the imposition of vicarious liability upon an enterprise.[134]

This response could equally be used to counteract those suggestions that an athlete's propensity for sexual violence is created only by their talent, rather than by their employment. Again, the more we believe that talent is the primary reason for, say, their expectation of access to women's bodies, the less justifiable it becomes to impose vicarious liability. However, we might once again conclude that it is a combination of these factors that gives rise to this risk. This can perhaps be demonstrated by the incident involving Manchester United footballer Harry Maguire, who was detained by Greek authorities after his involvement in a brawl on the island of Mykonos in August 2020. In an apparent attempt to avoid further punishment for his action, Maguire is alleged to have said: 'Do you know who I am? I am the captain of Manchester United, I am very rich, I can give you money... please let us go'.[135] However, if indeed talent was the *only* reason for a professional athlete's expectation of being above the law, then surely a more apt suggestion to the Greek authorities would have been 'I'm a very good footballer and I can give you money'?

To a large extent, we may never truly know just how significant the institutional and individual factors are in each case. Given the inherently discretionary nature of this area of law, it is clear that reasonable judicial minds may differ on this issue, particularly as Foster notes that the language of 'material contribution' can take on different meanings in different contexts.[136] However, I hope that I have done enough in this chapter to illustrate that, in most cases, an athlete's employment will constitute a more-than-negligible cause of their off-the-field sexual violence.

Conclusion

The somewhat unique nature of the celebrity tortfeasor has yet to be considered in UK case law on vicarious liability, and it has been illustrated here how a risk-based approach – based on insights from the law on privacy and unfair dismissal – could help to provide a satisfactory remedy for sexual harm caused by such individuals. In outlining that various socio-legal and interdisciplinary fields could be utilised to help inform the scope of employer liability, it has been shown how research on gendered violence – and in particular, insights from masculinity studies and feminist theory – could help to shape a risk-based approach in the professional (although not necessarily amateur) sports context. This was illustrated with reference to two overlapping off-the-field contexts: the sexual abuse of rookie athletes during hazing and initiation rituals, and the sexual assault of women.

In relation to the former, it was contended that it may be both normatively and empirically appropriate to impose liability on professional sports clubs for many acts of sexual hazing that occur away from the sports field. The analysis of *GB* illustrated how the adoption of an interdisciplinary, risk-based approach to vicarious liability could lead to more desirable results in practice. The concept of masculinities studies, which draws on the notions of power and authority that seemed to underpin the so-called 'tailored' approach in sexual abuse cases, could have been utilised to demonstrate how toxic masculinity is embedded into the fabric of many professional sports.

Likewise, with regard to the sexual assault of women away from the field, feminist legal theory ought to be employed to help expose the fact that the organisational conditions of professional sport arguably increase the risk of athletes committing such harm. This is reflected in the misogynistic subculture of many sports, as well as by the erroneous belief held by some athletes that they are entitled to easy sexual access to women's bodies. After demonstrating how these normative arguments could be reinforced by empirical data from the US, it was suggested in this chapter that sexual harm against women was not merely a coincidental risk of professional sport; rather, it was argued that the various institutional factors mentioned above may be operating as a material contribution to the injuries that victims suffer.

Notes

1   Josh Halliday, 'Adam Johnson Jailed for Six Years for Sexual Activity with Schoolgirl' (*The Guardian*, 24 March 2016) <https://www.theguardian.com/uk-news/2016/mar/24/adam-johnson-should-be-jailed-for-up-to-10-years-court-told>. See also *R v Johnson* [2017] EWCA Crim 191, [42].
2   Sarah Baxter, 'It's Game Over for Adam Johnson but Ched Evans Deserves a Replay' (*The Times*, 06 March 2016) <https://www.thetimes.co.uk/article/rightly-its-game-over-for-adam-johnson-but-ched-evans-deserves-another-shot-k9cffzcm7>.
3   Josh Halliday, 'Adam Johnson's Arrogance Led to Child Sexual Assault, Court Told' (*The Guardian*, 12 February 2016) <https://www.theguardian.com/uk-news/2016/feb/12/adam-johnsons-arrogance-led-to-child-sexual-assault-court-told>.
4   *R v Adam Johnson*, Sentencing Remarks of HHJ Rose (Bradford Crown Court, 24th March 2016), <https://www.judiciary.uk/wp-content/uploads/2016/03/r-v-johnson-sentencing.pdf>.
5   BBC, 'Adam Johnson Jailed for Six Years' (*BBC News*, 24 March 2016) <https://www.bbc.co.uk/news/uk-england-35891143>.
6   See, e.g., BBC, 'France Footballer Wissam Ben Yedder Charged with Rape' (*BBC News*, 11 August 2023) <https://www.bbc.co.uk/news/world-europe-66478622>; BBC, 'England Rugby International Arrested on Suspicion of Raping A Teenager' (*BBC News*, 12 January 2022) <https://www.bbc.co.uk/sport/rugby-union/59967847>.
7   Tim Fernandez and Kelly Fuller, 'A Scandal Every 22 Days: ARLC Hits Back Over Fresh de Belin Federal Court Challenge' (*ABC News*, 30 July 2019) <https://www.abc.net.au/news/2019-07-30/de-belin-federal-court-arlc-response/11367644>.
8   Evans' conviction was later quashed in *R v Evans* [2016] EWCA Crim 452.
9   BBC, 'Tyrell Robinson and Korie Berman Jailed for Sexual Activity with Children' (*BBC News*, 26 January 2021) <https://www.bbc.co.uk/news/uk-england-leeds-55817131>.
10 Despite being released from prison in March 2019, Johnson never resumed his professional career. This is likely due to the negative publicity that a club would receive for employing such a tainted player. See, e.g., Owen Gibson, 'Ched Evans Deal Called off Following Pressure on Oldham Athletic' (*The Guardian*, 08 January 2015) <https://www.theguardian.com/football/2015/jan/08/ched-evans-signing-called-off-oldham>.
11 For a sporting example in which the limitation period was disapplied, see *Blackpool Football Club Ltd v DSN* [2021] EWCA Civ 1352. In illustrating the fact-sensitive nature of this enquiry, however, it is noteworthy that it was not considered fair or just to disapply the limitation period in *TVZ & others v Manchester City Football Club Ltd* [2021] EWHC 1179 (QB).
12 Kyle Carlson et al., 'Bankruptcy Rates Among NFL Players with Short-Lived Income Spikes' (2015) 105 Am Econ Rev 381 (highlighting that almost 16% of NFL players were bankrupt within 12 years of retirement).
13 [2015] EWHC 2862 (QB).
14 See, e.g., Tom Dart, 'Why NBA Stars like James Harden and LeBron James Invest in Soccer Clubs' (*The Guardian*, 22 July 2019) <https://www.theguardian.com/sport/2019/jul/22/why-nba-stars-like-james-harden-and-lebron-james-invest-in-football-clubs?CMP=share_btn_tw> (noting that, in July 2019, basketballer James Harden had over 10 times as many Twitter followers as his former employer, the Houston Dynamos).
15 Gary Whannel, *Media Sports Stars: Masculinities and Moralities* (Routledge 2002) 145. See also Giuseppe Carabetta, 'Off-Duty Misconduct and the Employment Relationship: A Review of the Case Law' (2021) 48 ABLR 497, 498–9.

16 See, e.g., Simon Boyes, 'Legal Protection of Athletes' Image Rights in the United Kingdom' (2015) 15 ISLJ 69, 70.

17 Steve Greenfield and Guy Osborn, *Regulating Football: Commodification, Consumption and the Law* (Pluto Press 2001) 102.

18 Simon Chadwick and Nick Burton, 'From Beckham to Ronaldo – Assessing the Nature of Football Player Brands' (2008) 1 Journal of Sponsorship 307; Peter Kelly and Christopher Hickey, "Bringing the Game into Disrepute': the Ben Cousins Saga, Sports Entertainment, Player Welfare and Surveillance in the Australian Football League' (2012) 3 Asia-Pac J Health, Sport Phys Educ 35, 43.

19 Dart (n 14).

20 [2011] EWHC 2454 (QB), [91] (referring to *Von Hannover v Germany*, App No 59320/00 (2005) 40 EHRR 1).

21 [2015] EWHC 2361 (QB), [20].

22 *Crowe v An Post* [2016] ELR 93, 97. For scholarly confirmation on this point, see: Simon Honeyball, *Honeyball & Bowers' Textbook on Employment Law* (14th edn, OUP 2016) 180–2; Gwyneth Pitt, *Employment Law* (9th edn, Sweet & Maxwell 2014) 308; David Cabrelli, *Employment Law in Context* (4th edn, OUP 2020) 662.

23 *Moore v C & A Modes* [1981] IRLR 71.

24 *Ziems v Prothonotary of the Supreme Court of New South Wales* [1957] 97 CLR 279, 289 (Fullagar J).

25 [2013] EWHC 2869 (QB).

26 [2002] 1 AC 215, [62] (Lord Hobhouse).

27 Astrid Sanders, 'The Law of Unfair Dismissal and Behaviour Outside Work' (2014) 34 LS 328, 337.

28 [1992] IRLR 362 (CA).

29 This distinction between *Lister* and *P* suggests to me that the establishment of a work/conduct nexus for unfair dismissal purposes appears to be concerned with the policy issue of whether the conduct interferes with the employee's suitability for the job. This is reinforced by the ACAS Code of Practice on Disciplinary and Grievance Procedures 2015, [31] <https://www.acas.org.uk/acas-code-of-practice-for-disciplinary-and-grievance-procedures/html>. In contrast, the nexus for the purposes of vicarious liability seems to be more focussed on assessing whether the tortious harm was an inherent risk of the industry. Arguably, this is a more restrictive test.

30 Michael Kimmel, 'Foreword' in Judith Gardiner (ed), *Masculinity Studies and Feminist Theory: New Directions* (Columbia University Press 2002) ix.

31 Alex Hobbs, 'Masculinity Studies and Literature' (2013) 10 Lit Compass 383, 383.

32 Mae Quinn, 'Feminist Legal Realism' (2012) 35 Harv JL & Gender 1, 13.

33 Andrew Altman, 'Legal Realism, Critical Legal Studies, and Dworkin' (1986) 15 Philos Public Aff 205, 207.

34 Ernest Weinrib, 'Legal Formalism' in Dennis Patterson (ed), *A Companion to Philosophy of Law and Legal Theory* (Blackwell 2010) 337.

35 Quinn (n 32) 13.

36 ibid. See also Ken Kress, 'Legal Indeterminacy' (1989) 77 CLR 283, 283 and Mark Tushnet, 'Some Current Controversies in Critical Legal Studies' (2011) 12 Ger Law J 290, 290.

37 Phillip Morgan, 'Vicarious Liability and the Beautiful Game – Liability for Professional and Amateur Footballers?' (2018) 38 LS 242, 248.

38 *GB* (n 13).

39 ibid [156].

40 ibid [138]-[141]. This was not to say, however, that this was 'the equivalent of a positive finding that no such assaults took place'. As His Honour noted, the 'absolute truth' was likely not revealed by this trial.

41 ibid [148], [161].

42 Morgan (n 37) 250. This suggests that only acts committed by the apprentice's coach would lead to liability.

43 *Mohamud v WM Morrisons Supermarkets plc* [2014] EWCA Civ 116, [46] (Treacy LJ); *Various Claimants v Catholic Child Welfare Society* [2012] UKSC 56, [86]–[7] (Lord Phillips).

44 *GB* (n 13), [161].

45 ibid [145].

46 [2021] EWCA Civ 356, [84].

47 [2023] UKSC 15, [58]. For a similar view, see also Allison Silink and Desmond Ryan, 'Twenty Years on from *Lister v Hesley Hall Ltd* – Is there Now a "Tailored Close Connection Test" for Vicarious Liability in Cases of Sexual Abuse, or Not?' (2022) 38 PN 15, 33.

48 *BXB v Watch Tower and Bible Tract Society of Pennsylvania* [2020] EWHC 156 (QB), [161]. See also *Bazley v Curry* [1999] 2 SCR 534, [44] (McLachlin J).

49 *GB* (n 13), [145].

50 *BXB* (n 48), [162]. See also McLachlin J's comments in *Bazley* (n 48), [44]: 'The more the employer encourages the employee to stand in a position of respect and suggests that the child should emulate and obey the employee, the more the risk may be enhanced.'

51 *Maga v Birmingham Roman Catholic Archdiocese Trustees* [2010] EWCA Civ 256; *JGE v English Province of Our Lady of Charity* [2013] QB 722; *CCWS* (n 43).

52 *Mary M v City of Los Angeles* 54 Cal 3d 202 (1991); *Bernard v Attorney-General of Jamaica* [2004] UKPC 47; *N v Chief Constable of Merseyside Police* [2006] EWHC 3041 (QB).

53 [1999] 2 SCR 570, [18].

54 *GB* (n 13), [161]. His Honour was seemingly once again persuaded by counsel for the defendant, when they stated, at [146], that the 'risk of friction or confrontation between different classes of employee [was] no more inherent in the club's business conducted at the Victoria Football Ground than in any other workplace.'

55 *BXB* (n 46), [96].

56 Jonah Bury, 'Non-Performing Inclusion: A Critique of the English Football Association's Action Plan on Homophobia in Football' (2015) 50 International Review for the Sociology of Sport 211, 212. See also Cara Carmichael Aitchison, *Sport and Gender Identities: Masculinities, Femininities and Sexualities* (Routledge 2007) 17.

57 Jonathan Salisbury and David Jackson, *Challenging Macho Values: Practical Ways of Working with Adolescent Boys* (Routledge 1996) 205.

58 Eric Anderson, *Inclusive Masculinity: The Changing Nature of Masculinities* (Routledge 2009) 27; Julie Konieczny, 'There's Nothing Worse than Losing to a Girl: An Analysis of Sex Segregation in American Youth Sports' (2020) 8 IJLSE 70, 81.

59 Michael Messner, *Power at Play: Sports and the Problem of Masculinity* (Beacon Press 1992) 151. See also Jimmy Sanderson et al., 'A Hero or Sissy? Exploring Media Framing of NFL Quarterbacks Injury Decisions' (2014) 4 Commun Sport 3, 6.

60 Deborah Brake, 'Sport and Masculinity: The Promise and Limits of Title IX' in Frank Cooper and Ann McGinley (eds), *Masculinities and the Law: A Multidimensional Approach* (NYU Press 2012) 209.

61 Steven Schacht, 'Misogyny On and Off the "Pitch": The Gendered World of Male Rugby Players' (1996) 10 Gend Soc 550, 551; Adi Adams, Eric Anderson and Mark McCormack, 'Establishing and Challenging Masculinity: The Influence of Gendered Discourses in Organized Sport' (2010) 29 J Lang Soc Psychol 278, 281.

62 Tal Peretz and Chris Vidmar, 'Men, Masculinities, and Gender-Based Violence: The Broadening Scope of Recent Research' (2021) 15 Sociol Compass 1, 3.

63 Lisa Mazzie, 'Michael Sam and the NFL Locker Room: How Masculinities Theory Explains the Way We View Gay Athletes' (2014) 25 Marq Sports L Rev 129, 137–9.

64 Curtis Fogel and Andrea Quinlan, 'Sexual Assault in the Locker Room: Sexually Violent Hazing in Canadian Sport' (2020) J Sexual Aggress 1, 13–4.

65 Aaron Belkin, *Bring me Men: Military Masculinity and the Benign Façade of American Empire, 1898–2001* (Hurst Publishers 2012) 83.

66 Adams, Anderson and McCormack (n 61) 280.

67 Brake (n 60) 222.

68 Jennifer Waldron, 'Degrading and Harming New Teammates During Hazing: "Athletes will be Athletes" in Melanie Lang (ed), *Routledge Handbook of Athlete Welfare* (Routledge 2020) 119.

69 Jamie Thompson, James Johnstone and Curt Banks, 'An Examination of Initiation Rituals in a UK Sporting Institution and the Impact on Group Development' (2018) 18 ESMQ 544, 544.

70 Jennifer Waldron, Quinten Lynn and Vikki Krane, 'Duct Tape, Icy Hot & Paddles: Narratives of Initiation onto US Male Sport Teams' (2011) 16 Sport Educ Soc 111, 113.

71 Karin Volkwein-Caplan and Gopal Sankaran, *Sexual Harassment in Sport: Impact, Issues, and Challenges* (Meyer & Meyer Sport 2002) 11.

72 *Ministry of Defence v Radclyffe* [2009] EWCA Civ 635, [11]. More recently, see *TPKN v Ministry of Defence* [2019] EWHC 1488 (QB) (Ministry of Defence held vicariously liable for rape committed by a member of the armed forces after a social event in Gibraltar).

73 See Jack Thorne, 'When Do Sport Teams' Initiation Ceremonies Cross Legal Boundaries? Part 1' (LawInSport, 17 July 2014) (describing how former Manchester United stars Gary Neville and David Beckham were subject to sexual initiations, with the former reportedly being forced to strip naked whilst having the club kit scratched in dubbin onto his skin with a wire brush).

74 See, e.g., Elizabeth Allan, David Kerschner and Jessica Payne, 'College Student Hazing Experiences, Attitudes, and Perceptions: Implications for Prevention' (2018) 56 J Stud Aff Res Pract 32; Jay Johnson et al., 'An Examination of Hazing in Canadian Intercollegiate Sports' (2018) 12 J Clin Sport Psychol 144; Elizabeth Allan and Mary Madden, 'Hazing in View: College Students at Risk' (Initial Findings from the National Study of Student Hazing, March 2008) <https://stophazing.org/wp-content/uploads/2020/12/hazing_in_view_study.pdf>.

75 Jennifer Waldron, 'Predictors of Mild Hazing, Severe Hazing, and Positive Initiation Rituals in Sport' (2015) 10 Int J Sports Sci Coach 1089, 1095.

76 Marisalva Favero et al., 'Hazing Violence: Practices of Domination and Coercion in Hazing in Portugal' (2018) 33 J Interpers Violence 1830.

77 David Kerschner and Elizabeth Allan, 'Examining the Nature and Extent of Hazing at Five NCAA Division III Institutions and Considering the Implications for Prevention' (2021) 7 J Amat Sport 95, 103.

78 Jennifer Waldron and Christopher Kowalski, 'Crossing the Line: Rites of Passage, Team Aspects, and Ambiguity of Hazing' (2009) 80 Res Q Exerc Sport 291, 296.

79 Marc Edelman, 'Will March Madness be NCAA's Last Dance Featuring Ama-teurism as it Knows It' (*Forbes*, 17 March 2021) <https://www.forbes.com/sites/marcedelman/2021/03/17/will-march-madness-2021-be-shamateurisms-last-dance/?sh=6b69084368a6>.

80 John Wolohan, 'The NCAA Cases: Is it Losing Its Hold on College Sports in the United States?' (LawInSport, 07 March 2013). See also John Wolohan, 'Paving the Way to Professionalism for College Athletes – A Review of California's Fair Pay for Play Act' (LawInSport, 20 September 2019) (noting the example of Syracuse University, which generated around $94m in revenue from athletics in 2017–18).

81 ibid.

82 Wes Gerrie, 'More than Just the Game: How Colleges and the NCAA are Violating their Student-Athletes' Rights of Publicity' (2018) 18 Tex Rev Ent & Sports L 111, 113.

83 Jocelyn Robinson, 'USA vs UK Collegiate Sports System' (*Masterclass Sports*) <https://www.masterclasstours.co.uk/blog/usa-vs-uk-collegiate-sports-system>

84 See, e.g., Jonathan Casper, Michael Pfahl and Mark McSherry, 'Athletics Department Awareness and Action Regarding the Environment: A Study of NCAA Athletics Department Sustainability Practices' (2012) 26 J Sport Manag 11.

85 HC Deb 08 October 2013, Vol 568, col 17WH (Mr Hugo Swire).

86 Jere Longman, 'Ashley Wagner's Account of Sexual Assault Shakes Figure Skating' (*New York Times*, 01 August 2019) <https://www.nytimes.com/2019/08/01/sports/ashley-wagner-sexual-assault.html>.

87 Lawrence Ostlere, 'British Cycling "Extremely Concerned" by Report Alleging Widespread Harassment of Women in the Sport' (*The Independent*, 22 August 2019) <https://www.independent.co.uk/sport/cycling/rouleur-report-sexual-harassment-abuse-british-cycling-uci-a9074916.html>.

88 Juliet Macur and John Branch, 'Pro Cheerleaders Say Groping and Sexual Harassment are Part of the Job' (*New York Times*, 10 April 2018) <https://www.nytimes.com/2018/04/10/sports/cheerleaders-nfl.html>.

89 Lee McGinnis, Julia McQuillan and Constance Chapple, 'I Just Want to Play: Women, Sexism, and Persistence in Golf' (2005) 29 J Sport Soc Issues 313.

90 John Williams and Gavin Hall, 'A Good Girl is Worth their Weight in Gold': Gender Relations in British Horseracing' (2020) 55 Int Rev Sociol Sport 453.

91 Jason Haynes, 'Sport, Sexual Violence and the Law: A Feminist Critique and Call to Action' (2023) 23 ISLJ 99, 104.

92 Mark Lunney, Donal Nolan, and Ken Oliphant, *Tort Law: Text and Materials* (6th edn, OUP 2017) 867.

93 For judicial support on this point, see: *Lister* (n 26), [44] (Lord Clyde); *Bellman v Northampton Recruitment* [2018] EWCA Civ 2214, [22] (Asplin LJ).

94 Notable perpetrators include: Kellen Winslow (convicted of raping an unconscious teen in 2003); Ray Rice (filmed knocking his fiancée unconscious in 2014); and Ben Roethlisberger (accused of sexually assaulting numerous women). The controversial wide receiver Antonio Brown has also been involved in several high-profile incidents (including rape, sexual assault and domestic abuse).

95 Press Association, 'Six Huddersfield Giants Players Arrested on Suspicion of Rape' (*The Guardian*, 20 January 2010) <https://www.theguardian.com/sport/2010/jan/20/huddersfield-giants-police-rape-allegations>.

96 Merrill Melnick, 'Male Athletes and Sexual Assault' (1992) 63 J Phys Educ Recreat Dance 32, 32; Todd Crosset et al., 'Male Student-Athletes Reported for Sexual Assault: A Survey of Campus Police Departments and Judicial Affairs Offices' (1995) 19 J Sport Soc Issues 126, 126.

97 Martha Chamallas, 'Vicarious Liability in Torts: The Sex Exception' (2013) 48 Val UL Rev 133, 160–6; Freya Kristjanson, 'Vicarious Liability for Sexual Assault' (1999) 19 Can Woman Stud 93, 100.

98 524 U.S. 775 (1998).

99 ibid 800.

100 ibid 803 (citing Susan Estrich, 'Sex at Work' (1991) 43 Stan L Rev 813, 854).

101 Associated Press, 'Broadcaster says NBA Coach Luke Walton Laughed at her During Alleged Assault' (*The Guardian*, 24 April 2019) <https://www.theguardian.com/sport/2019/apr/24/luke-walton-kelli-tennant-assault-allegations-nba>.

102 Michael Flood and Sue Dyson, 'Sport, Athletes, and Violence Against Women' (2007) 4 NTV J 37, 40. See also Timothy Davis and Tonya Parker, 'Student-Athlete Sexual Violence against Women: Defining the Limits of Institutional Responsibility' (1998) 55 Wash Lee Law Rev 55, 65.

103 Chelsea Augelli and Tamara Kuennen, 'Domestic Violence & Men's Professional Sports: Advancing the Ball' (2018) 21 U Denv Sports & Ent LJ 27, 87.

104 See, e.g., Timothy Curry, 'Fraternal Bonding in the Locker Room: A Profeminist Analysis of Talk about Competition and Women' (1991) 8 Sociol Sport J 119; Mariah Nelson, *The Stronger Women Get, The More Men Love Football: Sexism and the American Culture of Sport* (Harcourt, Brace and Co 1994) 88; Ben Clayton and Barbara Humberstone, 'Men's Talk: A (Pro)feminist Analysis of Male University Football Players' Discourse' (2006) 41 Int Rev Sociol Sport 295.

105 Schacht (n 61) 558.

106 Peggy Reeves Sanday, 'The Socio-Cultural Context of Rape: A Cross-Cultural Study' (1981) 37 J Soc Issues 5, 25–6; Deborah Brake, 'Lessons from the Gender Equality Movement: Using Title IX to Foster Inclusive Masculinities in Men's Sport' (2016) 34 Law & Inequality 285, 302.

107 Bruce Kidd, 'The Men's Cultural Centre: Sports and the Dynamic of Women's Oppression/Men's Repression' in Michael Messner and Donald Sabo (eds), *Sport, Men, and the Gender Order* (Human Kinetics 1990) 42.

108 Eric Anderson, '"I Used to Think Women Were Weak": Orthodox Masculinity, Gender Segregation, and Sport' (2008) 23 Sociol Forum 257, 274–5.

109 Curtis Fogel, 'Precarious Masculinity and Rape Culture in Canadian University Sport' in Elizabeth Quinlan et al. (eds), *Sexual Violence at Canadian Universities: Activism, Institutional Responses, and Strategies for Change* (Wilfred Laurier University Press 2017) 152.

110 Christina Dardis et al, 'An Investigation of the Tenets of Social Norms Theory as They Relate to Sexually Aggressive Attitudes and Sexual Assault Perpetration: A Comparison of Men and Their Friends' (2015) 6 Psychol Violence 163.

111 William Beaver, 'College Athletes and Sexual Assault' (2019) 56 Society 620, 622 (referring to Jessica Luther, *Unsportsmanlike Conduct: Football and the Politics of Rape* (Akashic Books 2016)).

112 Jessica Woodhams, 'Leadership in Multiple Perpetrator Stranger Rape' (2012) 27 J Interpers Violence 728, 729. She notes that a broadly similar estimate of multiple perpetrator rapes (between 7–23%) is evident in the UK population.

113 Thomas Jackson and Joanne Davis, Prevention of Sexual and Physical Assault Toward Women: A Program for Male Athletes' (2000) 28 J Community Psychol 589, 592.

114 BBC, 'Alex Hepburn's Rape Conviction Upheld at Court of Appeal' (*BBC News*, 30 June 2020) <https://www.bbc.co.uk/news/uk-england-hereford-worcester-53231524>.

115 Alan Dundes, 'Into the Endzone for a Touchdown: A Psychoanalytic Consideration of American Football' (1978) 37 West Folk 75, 86.

116   Deborah Brake, 'The Struggle for Sex Equality in Sport and the Theory Behind Title IX' (2001) 34 U Mich J L Reform 13, 94; Deborah Brake, 'Going Outside Title IX to Keep Coach-Athlete Relationships in Bounds' (2012) 22 Marq Sports L Rev 395, 404.

117   As cited in Stanley Teitelbaum, *Sports Heroes, Fallen Idols* (University of Nebraska Press 2008) 24.

118   James Ducker, 'Johnson 'Knew he was Committing Child Sex Offence' (*The Times*, 12 February 2016) <https://www.thetimes.co.uk/article/johnson-knew-he-was-committing-child-sex-offence-ngds9h60g>.

119   David Goldblatt, *The Games: A Global History of the Olympics* (WW Norton Company 2016) 109–10.

120   Gayle Brewer and Sharon Howarth, 'Sport, Attractiveness, and Aggression' (2012) 53 Pers Individ Differ 640.

121   Brake (n 60) 212.

122   See Richard Haddad, 'Shield or Sieve – *People v Bryant* and the Rape Shield Law in High-Profile Cases' (2005) 39 Colum J Law & Soc Probs 185, 185–8.

123   Deb Waterhouse-Watson, 'News Media on Trial: Towards a Feminist Ethics of Reporting Footballer Sexual Assault Trials' (2016) 16 Fem Media Stud 952, 953.

124   See, e.g., Mary Frintner and Laurna Rubinson, 'Acquaintance Rape: The Influence of Alcohol, Fraternity Membership, and Sports Team Membership' (1993) 19 J Sex Educ Ther 272 (finding that 20.2% of males involved in sexual assault were sports team members, despite athlete making up less than 2% of the campus population); Crosset et al. (n 96) (finding that athletes made up only 3.7% of males at the surveyed universities, but were responsible for 19% of all sexual assaults).

125   Belinda-Rose Young et al., 'Sexual Coercion Practices Among Undergraduate Male Recreational Athletes, Intercollegiate Athletes, and Non-Athletes' (2017) 23 Violence Against Women 795, 803–4.

126   Kenny Jacoby, 'College Athletes More Likely to be Disciplined for Sex Assault' (*USA Today*, 12 December 2019) <https://eu.usatoday.com/in-depth/news/investigations/2019/12/12/ncaa-athletes-more-likely-disciplined-sex-assault/4379153002/>.

127   Robin Sawyer, Estina Thompson and Anne Chicorelli, 'Rape Myth Acceptance among Intercollegiate Student Athletes: A Preliminary Examination' (2002) 18 Am J Health Stud 19; Sarah Murnen and Marla Kohlman, 'Athletic Participation, Fraternity Membership, and Sexual Aggression among College Men: A Meta-Analytic Review' (2007) 57 Sex Roles 145.

128   Lise Wade, 'Rape on Campus: Athletes, Status, and the Sexual Assault Crisis' (*The Conversation*, 07 March 2017) <https://theconversation.com/rape-on-campus-athletes-status-and-the-sexual-assault-crisis-72255>.

129   Kristy McCray, 'Intercollegiate Athletes and Sexual Violence: A Review of Literature and Recommendations for Future Study' (2015) 16 Trauma, Violence, & Abuse 438, 440.

130   *South Australian Asset Management Corporation v York Montague Ltd* [1996] UKHL 10.

131   Margaret Hall, 'After Waterhouse: Vicarious Liability and the Tort of Institutional Abuse' (2000) 22 J Soc Welf Fam Law 159, 162.

132   *Jacobi* (n 53), [79]. This test was later applied by Lord Neuberger in *Maga* (n 51), [53].

133   See, e.g., *Bonnington Castings Ltd v Wardlaw* [1956] AC 613, 621 (Lord Reid); *Bailey v Ministry of Defence* [2009] 1 WLR 1052, 1068 (Waller LJ).

134   Alan Sykes, 'The Boundaries of Vicarious Liability: An Economic Analysis of the Scope of Employment Rule and Related Legal Doctrines' (1988) 101 Harv L Rev 563, 572–5.

135 Jack Rathborn, 'Harry Maguire Trial: Manchester United Captain asked Police 'Do you know who I am?' after Alleged Assault, Court Hears' (*The Independent*, 25 August 2020) <https://www.independent.co.uk/sport/football/premier-league/harry-maguire-trial-assault-police-greece-mykonos-bribery-court-a9687416.html>. Although Maguire has denied these accusations of bribery, Laurie Robinson, 'Professional Athletes – Held to a Higher Standard and Above the Law: A Comment on High-Profile Criminal Defendants and the Need for States to Establish High-Profile Courts' (1998) 73 Ind LJ 1313, 1331 observes that it is common practice amongst wrongdoing athletes to excuse their off-the-field behaviour by declaring: "Officer, I play for the…".

136 Neil Foster, 'Material Contribution in *Bonnington*: Not an Exception to 'But For' Causation' (2022) 49 UWAL Rev 404, 422–3.

5 Vicarious Liability for Off-the-Field Acts

Role Models, Disrepute Clauses and Concluding Guidance

Introduction

This chapter builds upon the argument made in Chapter 4, and it aims to assess whether the risk-based analysis in the previous chapter could be supplemented by various other considerations. It begins by exploring whether vicarious liability for off-the-field acts could be predicated on the fact that professional athletes are required to act as role models and brand ambassadors for their sport. Although this suggestion is implicit in the very small handful of works that have touched upon the scope of liability for athletes' extramural behaviour, it is argued here that this suggestion is far too wide and open-ended to be considered a satisfactory indicator of employer liability. The definition of a 'role model' is inherently vague, and the adoption of this approach is likely to lead to an illimitable scope of liability which would be out of step with the analysis offered in previous chapters. It is concluded that, if the role model status of a professional athlete is relevant at all, then it is only because it can go towards establishing a fairness-based justification for vicarious liability.

Consequently, the chapter then investigates this fairness rationale in more detail, and it explores how the role model status of professional athletes could potentially give rise to a benefit enterprise liability justification in this context. The idea here is simple: since clubs and governing bodies often seek to benefit from an athlete's fame and success through the imposition of overly intrusive contractual disrepute clauses, it is fair for them to also bear the burden of any foreseeable risks of harm. One important aspect of this analysis is the crucial distinction that ought to be drawn between acts that are intended to actively contribute to the positive reputation of a club, and acts that provide no immediate benefit to a club but still tarnish their reputation. Furthermore, and with one eye on the overlap between the theories of control and enterprise liability, it is maintained that employers may wish to reconsider their use of such widespread disrepute clauses if they wish to minimise their chances of being held strictly liable for off-the-field harm.

In the final section, I provide six guiding factors that judges may wish to consider when attempting to apply the close connection test for off-the-field

DOI: 10.4324/9781032665870-5

acts. This guidance draws on the analysis of the risk and benefit theories provided in this (and the previous) chapter, and it suggests that vicarious liability for extramural behaviour ought to be decided by balancing the following factors: the physicality of the sport played by the perpetrator; whether the wrongdoer participates in a team or individual sport; the popularity of the sport; the tortfeasor's on-field position; the type of act; and whether the wrongful act committed by the tortfeasor stemmed from an activity which benefitted the employer. In outlining this guidance, it will be demonstrated that a truly fact-specific, contextual approach is needed when determining the appropriate scope of vicarious liability for off-the-field conduct.

The Futility of a Role Model-Based Approach

It might be thought to be somewhat of a strawman argument to even suggest that a sports club ought to be held vicariously liable for extramural behaviour simply because their athletes have a responsibility to act as a role model away from the field. However, this possibility should not be overlooked. Of the three articles that very briefly touch upon the issue of vicarious liability for criminal off-the-pitch conduct by professional sportsmen, two make reference to an athlete's role model status in discussing the course of employment test in this context.[1] In fact, McCallum even observes that it is unclear how far vicarious liability could extend for private behaviour in light of the fact that professional athletes 'not only have responsibilities on the pitch but also off the pitch, as an ambassador of the clubs who employ them'.[2] This is reinforced by the views of some athletes themselves, when they suggest that being a role model away from the sport is part of their job.[3] My aim in this section is to illustrate why the imposition of vicarious liability based predominantly upon their status as role models should be avoided. In making this argument, I outline two reasons as to why this approach might give rise to an overly broad and indeterminate doctrine of vicarious liability.

The first can be exemplified with reference to *Jacobi v Griffiths*, a case in which the Canadian Supreme Court refused to find a recreational boys' and girls' club vicariously liable for the sexual assault perpetrated by an employee whom the club had held out to be 'a trusted confidant and role model'.[4] Here, Binnie J feared that, if liability were to be found, it would mean that all organisations providing positive role models to children would be subject to no-fault liability if their employees committed sexual abuse.[5]

This is an understandable concern in light of the wide-ranging definitions that are used to define 'role modelling'. According to Yancey, for instance, '[a] role model is an individual perceived as exemplary, or worthy of imitation'.[6] Other scholars adopt a similar two-pronged definition of role model status, which they say is attributable to both outstanding achievement and the ability to motivate others to adapt their behaviour.[7] Given the multitude of individuals that might legitimately fit these requirements – which may range from a university student acting as an ambassador at an open day, to the Prime Minister of a country – it seems reasonable to avoid resort to the 'somewhat ubiquitous' language of role modelling to determine the boundaries of vicarious liability.[8] After all, and as Addis posits, due to the malleable nature of the term, the rhetoric of 'role modelling' is often invoked by commentators as a fig leaf to make conclusory normative claims, rather than providing a distinct method of analysis *for* that claim.[9] Without some underlying theoretical guidance on the definition of a 'role model', we risk the law descending into an arbitrary mess of rules.

The second (related) reason for rejecting a role model-based approach is that it would lead to a potentially illimitable number of acts satisfying the course of employment enquiry. If we assume that professional athletes *are* role models – and UK privacy case law would suggest that this is the case[10] – then a close connection could be found in every scenario involving off-the-field misconduct by a sportsman. Although this would be consistent with the (implausible) view that professional athletes are '24 hours a day, 7 days a week' employees who must constantly act as brand ambassadors for their club,[11] it arguably sits uneasily alongside the findings made in previous chapters. After all, there is perhaps little wisdom in a model of vicarious liability that purports to impose responsibility on clubs for every harmful act committed away from the field whilst simultaneously maintaining that only certain acts *on*-the-field could give rise to a similar form of liability.

Of course, this concern might be appeased by adopting the view of scholars such as Feezell and Spurgin, who suggest that an athlete is only a role model within the limited confines of the sport they play (i.e. for their on-pitch exploits), *unless they actively seek out a role as a social influencer*.[12] On this basis, we might say that someone like Marcus Rashford – who has recently been instrumental in campaigning against the UK government's policy on free school meals – is a role model in the 'broader' sense of the word, and can justifiably be viewed as a 'moral exemplar' outside of his limited sphere of existence on the football pitch.[13] However, there appears to be something fundamentally illogical with tying this conception of role modelling to vicarious liability. From the victim's perspective (who is likely to have idolised the wrongdoer regardless), it seems absurd that their potential compensation could be dictated by an athlete's voluntary self-determination as to whether they are a social influencer or not. It perhaps mattered very little to Adam Johnson's victim whether or not the Sunderland player was advocating some form of social change.

Likewise, we might also question just how wide the scope of vicarious liability would be under this formulation. If Marcus Rashford is an activist for eliminating child poverty, does this mean that vicarious liability could only be imposed for any off-the-field act he committed which is intrinsically related to this work? Recent case law suggests that the answer to this question is 'yes',[14] so the fact that Rashford is a role model in the broader sense of the word would still not be enough to hold his employer (Manchester United) liable for, say, his sexual abuse of a woman. Lastly, it must be recognised that, if vicarious liability is predicated on an athlete's role as a social influencer, it would only be natural for clubs to dissuade their employees from engaging in such work (at great cost to society) in order to avoid the potential for liability.

What this discussion highlights is that the scope of the close connection test in the off-field context should not be based primarily on whether or not a professional athlete is a role model and/or brand ambassador. This approach is likely to lead to an illimitable scope of liability, and it would almost certainly be rejected following the (overly) restrictive application of vicarious liability advocated by the Supreme Court in *Barclays Bank v Various Claimants*[15] and *WM Morrison Supermarkets v Various Claimants*.[16] In contrast, the advantage of the risk-based method perused in the previous chapter is that, whilst it is still undoubtedly broader than the approach envisioned by the Supreme Court in *Barclays* and *Morrison*, it does still contain *some* limits to liability (as discussed in the concluding guidance at the end of this chapter).

As such, if an athlete's status as a role model is relevant at all, then it ought to be viewed from a legal and contractual perspective, rather than, as much of the literature on this issue has previously done, through a moral or philosophical lens. Indeed, surely the best starting point in determining whether an athlete was acting within the course of their employment is to examine what the employer was demanding of their employee in the first place.[17] When this vantage point is adopted, we see that the existence of disrepute clauses in many professional sporting contracts may provide an interesting benefit enterprise liability justification for vicarious liability that could work in tandem with the risk-based approach outlined in the previous chapter.

Disrepute Clauses and the Close Connection Test

As has been made clear by the jurisprudence of the Court of Arbitration for Sport ('CAS'), sporting disrepute clauses – or, as they have otherwise been termed, 'morals clauses' – are intrinsically linked to the perceived notion that a professional athlete is both 'a leader and a role model' within the community.[18] These clauses are commonly found in many contracts in the entertainment industry,[19] and they have equally been described as 'ubiquitous' in the sports sector.[20] Whilst the first example of such a provision occurred in 1922 in an attempt to regulate the off-field conduct of the legendary baseballer Babe Ruth,[21] the rapid commercialisation of professional sport has meant that it is now common practice for clubs to incorporate disrepute clauses into every contract offered to an athlete. Indeed, the collective bargaining agreements in the four major US sporting leagues – the NFL, NBA, MLB and NHL – all contain a 'standard player agreement that include(s) a morals clause'.[22] Likewise, in the UK, both the Premier League[23] and the Gallagher Premiership[24] utilise standard playing contracts that include provisions forbidding athletes from bringing their employers or their sport into disrepute.

A fine example of a disrepute clause in action can be seen in reference to the recent controversy surrounding the English rugby union player Danny Cipriani, who was found guilty of assaulting a bouncer and resisting arrest outside a nightclub in 2018. The Rugby Football Union (RFU) subsequently charged Cipriani with 'conduct prejudicial to the interest of the game' under rule 5.12 of the RFU's Membership rules,[25] and the independent disciplinary panel reiterated that, as a role model, Cipirani was 'expected to behave in line with the core values of the game which include respect and discipline'.[26] Similar wording is also evident in the rulebooks of some individual sports,[27] as well as in the tortfeasor's contract in *Gravil v Carroll and Redruth Rugby Football Club*. As noted in Clarke MR's judgment in this case, the semi-professional rugby union player here had been required to 'observe the highest standards in his conduct both on and off the field' so that he did not 'bring the club, the RFU or rugby into disrepute'.[28]

The Practical Significance of Disrepute Clauses: Sport and Beyond

In light of the widespread ubiquity of disrepute clauses, one might make a number of interesting practical observations about these contractual provisions. First, given that such disrepute clauses are often included for the benefit of both clubs *and* governing bodies, it seems that dual vicarious liability may be appropriate in responding to the off-field actions of athletes who participate in team sports.[29] This is consistent with the argument I make elsewhere that we ought to consider imposing dual vicarious liability more frequently in the sporting context.[30] Furthermore, imposing dual vicarious liability also reflects the fact that many of the normative risk factors outlined in the previous chapter – such as toxic masculine subcultures and a perceived entitlement to women – are actually intrinsic risks created by particular sports as a whole, rather than by individual clubs *within* that sport.

In this regard, and in addition to the liability of clubs, it is perhaps desirable in this context to also impose vicarious liability on regulatory bodies and competition organisers as a proxy for sector liability. Whether such a conclusion could equally justify the imposition of strict liability on other stakeholders with a vested interest in the off-the-field behaviour of athletes – such as advertisers and sponsors who rely on disrepute clauses to unilaterally terminate an agreement with an athlete who 'engages in reprehensible behaviour or conduct that may negatively impact his or her public image'[31] – is less clear. In this instance, it would need to be shown that such a company satisfies the stage one relationship test.[32] If they do, it may also be possible to include them as a defendant in a vicarious liability claim for off-the-field harm.

Second, and in light of the fact that disrepute clauses are utilised in a variety of other industries, one might question whether my argument in this chapter proves too much. Indeed, one could point to the various risk factors of sexual assault, and argue that they similarly apply to numerous other industries in which morals clauses are used. For example, misogynistic language and hierarchies of masculinity are arguably a feature of the legal profession,[33] and it might also be suggested that this is an industry that is equally replete with competitive streaks and a winner-loser dichotomy. Likewise, a perceived entitlement to women as a result of fame and success seemingly applies just as much to musicians and film stars, whilst the physically aggressive nature of professional sport perhaps pales in comparison to the military. However, what is striking here is that in no other industry are the *conglomeration* of these factors quite as strong as in sport. Working in a law firm, for instance, does not entail any physical aggression as part of its role. In contrast, whilst military personnel *are* required to use violence, the lack of celebrity status for such individuals means that the risk factor of easy sexual access to women is not as strong here as in sport.

Of course, this is not necessarily to say that all of the risk factors for sexual abuse highlighted in the previous chapter need to be satisfied before imposing vicarious liability. After all, the guidance I provide to judges later in this chapter is not intended to act as a checklist or box-ticking exercise. What it does illustrate, though, is that the justification for vicarious liability in some professional sports is arguably stronger than in most – if not all – other industries that possess similar risk factors. In this light, whilst my discussion in this chapter perhaps ought to send a salutary warning to other enterprises about the possibility of vicarious liability for extramural behaviour, the context-sensitive approach adopted here means that this analysis should only ever be instructive (rather than determinative) for these other sectors. This is reinforced by the fact that any purported increased risk of sexual violence in these other industries ideally ought to be empirically validated, as well as by the fact that the relationship test at stage one would also need to be satisfied (which may, for instance, rule out vicarious liability for truly independent film stars or musicians). Framed in this way, the possibility of indeterminate (or overly broad) liability is significantly diminished.

Third, and to return more specifically to the issue of disrepute clauses, it is clear that, in practice, these contractual provisions cover a much wider range of behaviour than sexual violence. In fact, they have been used to sanction athletes involved in (amongst other things) drink driving, discrimination, kidnapping and assault cases.[34] Clearly, not all of these acts will give rise to vicarious liability under a risk-based approach. As such, the benefit enterprise liability justification perused here will need to work harmoniously alongside the risk-based argument outlined in the previous chapter. I have previously explored the need for some consistency between these two strands of enterprise liability,[35] and I aim to develop this point further in this chapter by showing how a fairness argument (based on the existence of disrepute clauses) can supplement the notion of risk in this context.

The Theoretical Significance of Disrepute Clauses: Benefit Enterprise Liability

The aim of this section is to sharpen the normative theoretical relevance of disrepute clauses to the imposition of vicarious liability. In particular, it could be said that, in line with comments made in *Cox v Ministry of Justice* and *Armes v Nottinghamshire County Council*, such clauses indicate that off-the-field torts are committed as a 'result of activity taken by the employee on behalf of the employer'.[36] Indeed, it seems that sports clubs – through a process known as 'meaning transference' – often seek to latch onto an athlete's 'established familiarity and credibility' to make their own enterprise more appealing to the public.[37] We could say that this was the point at the heart of the Cipriani case, in that the RFU was seeking to transfer the perceived ideals of respect and discipline (two fundamental traits of any professional sportsman) from Cipriani to the organisation. On this basis, it is arguable that sports stars are only required to behave in an orderly manner away from the field *because it serves the interests of their employer.*

Likewise, and to further reiterate this point, the existence of disrepute clauses also demonstrates that off-the-field conduct could be classed as part of the employer's business activity.[38] According to Lord Reed in *Cox*, this requirement is concerned with the so-called 'fairness' aspect of enterprise liability:

> since the employee's activities are undertaken as part of the activities of the employer and for its benefit, it is appropriate that the employer should bear the cost of harm wrongfully done by the employee within the field of activities assigned to him.[39]

This can be illustrated with reference to the world-renowned footballer Cristiano Ronaldo, whose transfer to Juventus in July 2018 was seemingly motivated just as much by the commercial and broadcasting opportunities that this opened up to his employer as it was by his on-field talent. In light of the so-called 'Ronaldo effect', the club's share price more than doubled following his signing, raising Juventus' market capitalisation to €1.5 billion.[40] The four-year contract offered by the club also allowed them to use his image rights in promotional campaigns for Juventus.[41] Given that '\$47 million of Ronaldo's estimated \$108 million earnings [in 2017] came from endorsements',[42] this was clearly a huge financial coup for the Italian club. In fact, the commercial value of the Ronaldo 'brand' was so great that, when Juventus travelled to Asia to participate in a pre-season friendly in 2019, South Korean fans threatened the club with legal action after they left the Portuguese striker on the bench for the entire game.[43]

Given, therefore, that Ronaldo's club was benefitting from his reputational and commercial success in this manner, it seems fair to maintain that they should also have to bear the consequences of any reasonably foreseeable harm that he might cause as part of this role. After all, the link between his off-field conduct and the reputation of Juventus was seemingly so stark that, when rape allegations were made against Ronaldo in 2018, the stock market valuation of his club plummeted by over €100 million.[44] In line with Lord Phillips' comments in *CCWS*,[45] this may serve to further reinforce the contention that Ronaldo's off-the-field conduct was intrinsically linked to the business activities of Juventus.

Now, it may be easy to assume that this is an atypical example in light of Ronaldo's widespread fame and exorbitant success. It may also be a rather unusual case insofar as the allegations which affected Juventus were reported to have occurred whilst Ronaldo was playing for Manchester United in 2009.[46] However, as illustrated by the facts of *Mason v Huddersfield Giants Ltd*,[47] this fairness-based reasoning could be equally applicable to other (more quintessential) examples involving professional sportsmen who do not possess the same celebrity status as Ronaldo.

As discussed in Chapter 4, the facts in *Mason* involved a picture of an individual's anus being posted on the claimant rugby player's social media account by one of his teammates. Due to the fact that the claimant was heavily intoxicated at the time, he failed to promptly remove this post. Although the subsequent dismissal of the athlete was held to be unfair, it had been argued by the defendant club that the tweet brought them into disrepute, as 'the club took advantage of those players who subscribed to Twitter by ensuring that they tweeted information about the club to their followers'.[48] But by the same logic, then, if a club is seeking to avail themselves of any financial (and/or public relations) benefit as a result of their employees' popularity, it is only fair that they should take responsibility – through the guise of vicarious liability – when an employee turns bad. In other words, sports employers should not be allowed to have their cake and eat it too by receiving any positive meaning transference whilst simultaneously being able to reject any negative meaning transference.

Mason is also interesting in that it highlights a potentially crucial distinction between acts that are intended to actively contribute to the positive reputation of an employer, and acts that provide no benefit to an employer but otherwise still tarnish their reputation. *Mason* is arguably an example of the former in that the player's use of social media was helping his club to build 'relationships with the community, families and children'.[49] Conversely, the alleged rape by Ronaldo is seemingly an example of the latter, as it was clearly not done in the context of providing any such benefit to his employer at the time. For these latter acts, it will likely be necessary for a fairness justification predicated on disrepute clauses to work alongside and supplement the risk-based approach outlined in the previous chapter.

In contrast, for those acts that are committed in the context of charity-led initiatives designed to proactively promote the status of their employer – such as those found in Clause 4 of the standard Premier League contract, which deals with the 'community, public relations and marketing' duties of athletes[50] – it may be that benefit enterprise liability could alone justify vicarious liability here, regardless of whether the act committed was an intrinsic risk of the sport. This could include, for instance, any tortious conduct that occurs in relation to signing autographs, engaging in charity work or visiting youth centres. This is reinforced by HHJ Butler's comments in *GB v Stoke City Football Club Ltd*, when he indicated that, if Peter Fox had assaulted a young fan in the course of performing his contractual obligation to act as the president of a youth fan club, then the club would probably have been held vicariously liable.[51] Consequently, this means that clubs and governing bodies in even the most genteel of non-contact sports – such as golf, snooker and volleyball – may still wish to seriously consider their potential liability for off-the-field conduct if they mandate engagement with any of these civic or social duties.

Importantly, it is perhaps worth examining how this analysis of fairness interacts with a risk-based approach when looking at acts that do not directly contribute to the positive reputation of an employer. The key point to remember here is that it is *not* strictly necessary for benefit and risk to point to the same conclusion on liability in order to determine an employer's responsibility for off-the-field injury. Rather, the point I make here is that if both benefit and risk are employed to determine the scope of the close connection test in this context, then they both need to be geared towards the same type of harm. In other words, whenever both forms of enterprise liability are raised as justifications for imposing or rejecting liability, it would not be desirable to apply risk-based reasoning to any act other than those from which the employer stood to benefit (and vice versa). This is a point that has previously been recognised by Bell, as he argues that both 'benefit and risk must be kept close together if an enterprise theory is to hold'.[52]

Three final points are relevant here. First, and as Flannigan outlines, there is a significant overlap between the theories of benefit and control.[53] This is important because the overly intrusive regulation associated with disrepute clauses perhaps further justifies the imposition of vicarious liability on sports employers. Indeed, because such clauses purport to make professional athletes 'answerable for all publicly known albeit private time conduct', Jonson,

Lynch and Adair have suggested that the current employment of sports stars is analogous to a '"master-servant" contract relationship typical of a bygone era, where the master owns the slave'.[54] Other scholars have likewise pointed out that disrepute provisions are also oftentimes used to silence athletes by stifling dissent and diversity of opinion.[55]

This is reinforced by the inordinate amount of discretion afforded to employers in deciding whether to sanction an athlete under a disrepute charge. According to the CAS panel in *D'Arcy v Australian Olympic Committee*, to bring an entity into disrepute is to lower its reputation 'in the eyes of ordinary members of the public to a significant extent'.[56] More recent judgments have clarified that it refers to the 'loss of reputation or dishonour'.[57] As we can see, disrepute clauses thus seem to be based predominantly on community standards and moral values, and the highly malleable nature of these concepts means that athletes are subjected to an unreasonable amount of control.[58] In this regard, it might well be suggested that if clubs are so eager to govern the actions of their players beyond the touchline, then they should equally be ready to assume responsibility for those actions when an individual misbehaves. After all, and as was highlighted by Lord Pearson in *Home Office v Dorset Yacht Co Ltd*, 'control imports responsibility'.[59]

Second, Davidson has suggested that the expansion of the doctrine of vicarious liability could explain why many employers have taken a more active interest in the off-duty conduct of their employees.[60] The contention here appears to be that, if an employer is at risk of being held strictly liable for a wider range of acts, then it is only rational for them to encroach upon their employees' private life in order to ensure that any particular individual is not likely to commit a tort. But by the same token, then, we might alternatively conclude that an increased attempt to control and regulate the off-duty behaviour of employees (as evidenced by such discretionary disrepute clauses) should normatively also lead to an increased scope of vicarious liability. This may be yet another example of how insights from the law on privacy and unfair dismissal could help us to determine the appropriate scope of employer liability in this context.

The third point is that, whilst sports clubs have long sought to take advantage of such ill-defined and pervasive disrepute provisions in an attempt to protect the good will and reputation of their brand, the analysis offered here demonstrates that these clauses could in fact function as a significant financial *disadvantage*, in that they potentially open employers up to a wider scope of vicarious liability. Of course, whether the potential exposure to liability generated by these clauses outweighs the benefits of inducing better off-the-field behaviour is an important empirical economic question for each club to assess. However, the discussion here highlights that many employers ought to reconsider incorporating such oppressive and unduly extensive clauses into their athletes' contracts.

In this regard, I must agree with Paterson when he suggests that disreputable conduct 'should be more clearly defined'.[61] Rather than simply relying on a condensed and amorphous disrepute charge, clubs should instead consider drafting separate and more precise contractual provisions in order to regulate specific off-the-field acts. This could work to benefit various stakeholders in sport, including the players (who will have a better idea about what conduct is, and is not, acceptable away from the pitch) and the clubs themselves (who could potentially limit their control over – and perhaps therefore their responsibility for – their employees to certain acts).

Concluding Guidance

With this (and the previous) chapter in mind, this concluding section offers six normative factors for judges to consider when translating the prior analysis into concrete practical guidance. This analysis reaffirms that a truly contextual and fact-sensitive approach is necessary to help us determine the scope of vicarious liability for off-the-field acts. As such, and largely in contrast to Lord Toulson's view in *Mohamud v WM Morrison Supermarkets Plc* (where he argued that measuring the closeness of connection on a scale of 1 to 10 would be a 'forlorn exercise'),[62] I suggest that vicarious liability in this context is perhaps best viewed in light of a spectrum-based approach. This will require judges to consider (and balance) the following six considerations, and it will likely be a matter of judicial discretion as to which factors a judge deems to be the most important in each case. Of course, some are likely to bemoan the potential uncertainty that this approach generates, but it is arguably no more uncertain than using the empty tags that judges already tend to rhetorically invoke when assessing risk (e.g. 'inherent risk'; 'reasonably incidental risk').[63]

Furthermore, a spectrum-based approach seems to be preferable to insisting on a specific increase in risk (such as the 'doubling of the risk' approach offered in some factual causation cases),[64] which is likely to result in an overly rigid application of vicarious liability. For example, an insistence on a 100% increase in the hazing statistics referred to in the previous chapter would mean that a finding of 49.5% of sports-related hazing (from a baseline of 24.8% for non-athletes) would not be enough to impose vicarious liability, whereas a finding of 49.7% would be.[65] It is highly doubtful whether such a strict approach is desirable, particularly in light of the different methodologies and definitions of hazing that might be used in each study.

Physical or Non-Contact Sport

Various scholars have identified the existence of a gendered hierarchy within male sport, such that athletes in certain sports are more prone to engaging in off-the-field violence.[66] One notable risk factor is participation in aggressive sports, and in particular the notion that being physically 'aggressive on the field is associated with having a strong sex drive'.[67] Forbes et al provide empirical support for this proposition, observing that males who partake in more physically invasive sports exhibited a higher level of sexual hostility towards women than athletes in other (less brutal) sports.[68] The latter games are more fixated on the accuracy and elegance of the participants, and this appears to give rise to a more 'refined' and 'genteel' masculinity that makes any off-the-field sexual assault less inherent to that enterprise.[69] Of course, fierce competitors and aggressive playing styles exist in even the most placid of sports (the golfer Sergio Garcia perhaps springs to mind here): however, the focus for this factor is on whether physicality and aggression are a necessary prerequisite to successful participation at the elite level of the sport (as it is, for instance, in rugby, ice hockey and American football).

Team or Individual Sport

Perhaps due to the need to constantly re-prove their masculine capital amongst peers, some commentators have similarly suggested that participation in team sports – as opposed to individual sports – further increases the risk of violent off-the-field behaviour.[70] This is perhaps unsurprising in light of the observation by feminist scholars in the previous chapter that suggest that many athletes are subjected to immense peer pressure to commit sexual violence against women. The alarmingly high number of gang rapes committed by athletes is seemingly testament to this fact.

In this light, one might identify a tension here in relation to combat sports, as they are both physically aggressive *and* an individual sport. However, the anomaly of combat sports perhaps only serves to reinforce the fact that the six considerations outlined here are only to be viewed as useful pointers for judges, and it is the *ensemble* of these factors that will help to shed light on whether a certain off-the-field risk is intrinsic to that sport or not. This will necessarily require judges to conduct a delicate balancing exercise. Many might, therefore, logically surmise that the overtly aggressive nature of combat sports outweighs the fact that it is not a team game, such that a governing body in the sport of, say, boxing, could plausibly be held liable for a boxer's extramural behaviour.

Popularity of the Sport

Empirical data suggests that athletes competing in what are termed 'centre sports' (i.e. sports that attract the most publicity and finances, such as football and basketball) are more likely to display sexually violent tendencies than those participants who compete in the less prominent 'marginal sports' (such as swimming or volleyball, for instance).[71] This is perhaps unsurprising given that athletes who play in the former are more likely to possess a greater sense of entitlement to the 'privileges' of their elite status. Moreover, within this centre-marginal framework, one may also wish to identify the level at which the tortfeasor plays: for example, the popularity of Premier League football is, of course, far greater than the popularity of League 2 football.

Tortfeasor's On-Field Position

On a related point, Welch observes that a propensity for off-the-field violence against women may even be directly linked to an individual's role *on*-the-field, with those players in the more prestigious roles – such as the running back in American football – more likely to harm women.[72] This could be due, in part, to the so-called 'winner effect', a biological phenomenon that suggests that testosterone levels increase following competitive success.[73] Gonzalez-Bono et al note, however, that changes to testosterone in team sports are not typically linked with the outcome of a sporting contest (i.e. a win or loss), but more with an individual's contribution to that outcome.[74] The greater the contribution one makes to their team's success, the higher their increase in testosterone is likely to be. Consequently, given that a game-winning goal or touchdown is more likely to be scored by a star player who occupies the most prestigious role, it may be useful to assess the tortfeasor's on-the-field position in determining vicarious liability for off-the-field sexual acts.[75]

Of course, it is worth reiterating that a participant's role on the field is not, by itself, a conclusive factor (and it may only be useful to help tip the balance in very borderline cases). Indeed, the fact that Peter Fox in *GB* occupied the arguably less prestigious role of goalkeeper ought not to necessarily rule out vicarious liability in this case given the overwhelming weight of other factors (such as the widespread popularity and masculine physicality of football).

Type of Act

As Judge Friendly remarked in *Ira S Bushey & Sons v United States*, vicarious liability does not 'reach into areas where the servant does not create risks different from those attendant on the activities of the community in general'.[76] Consequently, and in addition to the above criteria, we must also take into account the nature of the wrongful act in deciding whether or not to impose vicarious liability. Interestingly, over a 14-year period between 2000 and 2013, NFL players had a much lower arrest rate for public order crimes – such as drink driving, public indecency and animal abuse – compared to the general population.[77] This suggests that NFL clubs ought not to be vicariously liable for, say, the fatal drink driving incident caused by Henry Ruggs in 2021,[78] or for Michael Vick's involvement in running an illegal dog-fighting ring in 2007.[79] In contrast, and despite the overall US population having a much higher arrest rate in general than NFL players, the rate of arrest for *violent crime* – which includes offences such as sexual assault, rape, battery and robbery – was 'significantly higher' among NFL players in many of the yearly comparisons.[80]

Of course, variations in this category of offences will differ, and it may be that some sexual acts are more intrinsically linked to a player's employment than other acts. In this regard, it may be instructive to adopt a similar spectrum-based approach to that utilised by Ouseley J in the privacy case of *Theakston v MGN Ltd*, where he highlighted that, whilst '[s]exual relations within marriage at home would be... protected from most forms of disclosure... a transitory engagement in a brothel' may not be.[81] Although Ouseley J's approach may no longer constitute good law on the reasonable expectation of privacy for sexual encounters,[82] his methodology may still be useful for our purposes here.

Benefit to the Employer

Finally, if it can be shown that an employer benefitted from an act that was also an inherent risk of a particular sport, then this further increases the desirability of imposing vicarious liability. For acts that are intended to directly contribute to the positive reputation of their club – such as the scenario in *Mason*, or indeed other civic duties that are expected of athletes – then benefit enterprise liability alone could justify imposing vicarious liability. For those acts that do not contribute to enhancing the reputation of the employer (such as, for instance, sexual abuse that was not facilitated by any community or public relations role), then it may be necessary for a risk-based approach to work alongside, and supplement, the benefit formulation of enterprise liability. In the absence of such an overlap, it must be recognised that any conclusion is significantly weakened from an enterprise liability perspective.

Applying the Guidance

On a brief concluding note, it may be useful to illustrate how this six-point guidance might be tentatively applied to some fictitious and real-life scenarios. At one end of the spectrum, where vicarious liability is most unlikely, we might find a lower-ranked golfer who commits domestic violence against his wife or long-term partner behind closed doors. Moving towards more borderline cases in the centre, we might see a budding young professional basketballer who sexually assaults a new lover in his apartment. At the furthest end of the spectrum (where liability is normatively most appropriate) is an elite international rugby player who, perhaps as part of a sexual conquest game between his teammates, rapes a woman in a hotel room where he is staying following an away game. In contrast to the golfer example, it is the inherently

misogynistic and violent subculture of professional rugby (as well as the athlete's perceived entitlement to certain sexual privileges resulting from his athletic success) that makes the latter scenario a more intrinsic risk of the sport.
This is supported by many of the empirical statistics referred to in this and the
previous chapter.

Following this analysis, then, we might conclude that Sunderland AFC
were arguably more likely than not to have been found vicariously liable for
Adam Johnson's sexual assault had his victim sought compensation. Johnson
was first introduced to his victim after signing an autograph for the young girl
outside of Sunderland's home ground, so this suggests that he was actively
contributing to the reputation of his employer (and conferring a benefit on
them). In addition, and from a risk-based perspective, Johnson was a successful attacking footballer who, at the time of the offence, played for a popular
Premier League club in a physically invasive team sport. As mentioned in the
previous chapter, his act was motivated by an arrogant expectation of access
to women, and the available empirical data appears to suggest that his employment as an elite professional footballer may have materially contributed
to the sexual assault of his victim in this incident.

Conclusion

This chapter highlighted that a risk-based approach to vicarious liability for
off-the-field acts was preferable to imposing liability on the basis that athletes are role models. Although this was a suggestion made in some of the
existing works on this topic, it is likely that this approach would lead to
liability for *every* off-the-field act (particularly if one is convinced by the
somewhat implausible argument that professional athletes are 24/7 brand
ambassadors). In contrast, an enterprise liability-based approach that focusses on risk and benefit would impose some limits on the scope of vicarious liability in this context. As such, even those in favour of the narrow
Barclays/Morrison approach to vicarious liability may find some merit in
the enterprise liability-based solution advocated in this book. It was further
contended that, if the role model status of a professional athlete is relevant at
all, then it should go towards establishing a fairness rationale for vicarious
liability in this context.

This suggestion was predicated on the ubiquity of disrepute clauses in
many professional sporting contracts, and in particular the notion that employers often seek to latch on to the reputational and sporting success of their
employees. In this regard, it was suggested that if sports clubs seek to take
advantage of any positive meaning transference generated by the off-field exploits of an athlete, then they should equally have to bear the costs of any
negative meaning transference if an athlete engages in reasonably foreseeable
harmful conduct. Although it is true that disrepute clauses are utilised in many

other industries besides sport, it was maintained that such an approach would not lead to overly broad liability. In addition, an important distinction was also drawn between acts that directly contribute to an employer's positive reputation, and acts that provide no benefit to an employer but still tarnish their reputation. For the former, benefit enterprise liability alone could perhaps justify vicarious liability; for the latter, a fairness rationale (based on disrepute clauses) may need to work alongside the risk-based approach outlined in the previous chapter.

With this in mind, the chapter concluded by offering six guiding considerations that judges may wish to examine in translating the prior discussion into practice. In line with a legal realist understanding of the law, it will necessarily be left to the discretion of each individual judge as to the precise weight to afford to each of these normative factors. As was illustrated by my final application of these factors to Adam Johnson's sexual abuse case, this guidance may help to produce an empirically-informed law on vicarious liability that is sensitive to context, theory and factual nuance.

Notes

1 Laura McCallum, 'An Overview of Key Case Law Relating to Negligent Liability for Sports Injuries (Part 1)' (LawInSport, 07 October 2016); Phillip Morgan, 'Vicarious Liability and the Beautiful Game – Liability for Professional and Amateur Footballers?' (2018) 38 LS 242, 248 (suggesting that there would be no vicarious liability for assault in a nightclub *despite the fact* that 'players are encouraged to be role models on and off the pitch'). The third article – Philip Hutchinson, 'Who Shoulders the Blame? An Analysis of Vicarious Liability in the Sports Industry' (LawInSport, 03 October 2016) – does not refer to the role model status of professional athletes, but this is likely because his focus here was on sexual misconduct at club-run charity events. Given that case law already supports vicarious liability in this scenario (see n 51), it was unnecessary for the author to delve into the scope of an athlete's obligations as an ambassador.
2 ibid.
3 Sandra Lynch, Daryl Adair and Paul Jonson, 'Professional Athletes and their Duty to be Role Models' in Arthur Caplan and Brendan Parent, *The Ethics of Sport: Essential Readings* (OUP 2017) 231 (outlining the views of former NBA star Karl Malone, who suggested that professional athletes cannot 'accept all the glory and the money that comes with being a famous athlete and not accept the responsibility of being a role model').
4 [1999] 2 SCR, [4].
5 ibid [82].
6 Antronette Yancey, 'Building Positive Self Image in Adolescents in Foster Care: The Use of Role Models in an Interactive Group Approach' (1998) 33 Adolescence 253, 256.
7 Pamela Wicker and Bernd Frick, 'The Inspirational Effect of Sporting Achievements and Potential Role Models in Football: A Gender-Specific Analysis' (2016) 21 Manag Sport Leis 265, 266.
8 *Ferdinand v MGN* [2011] EWHC 2454 (QB), [87] (Nicol J).
9 Adeno Addis, 'Role Models and the Politics of Recognition' (1996) 144 U Pa L Rev 1377, 1455.

10 *A v B* [2003] QB 195, [43] (Lord Woolf); *Ferdinand* (n 8), [90] (Nicol J); *Jackson v BBC* [2017] NIQB, [64] (Keegan J).

11 Glen Bartlett and Regan Sterry, 'Regulating the Private Conduct of Employees' (2012) 7 ANZSLJ 91, 105. For a more sensible view, see Paul Horvath, 'Anti-Doping and Human Rights in Sport: The Case of the AFL and the *WADA* Code' (2006) 32 Mon LR 357, 375.

12 Randolph Feezell, 'Celebrated Athletes, Moral Exemplars, and Lusory Objects' (2005) 32 J Philos Sport 20; Earl Spurgin, 'Hey, How Did *I* Become a Role Model? Privacy and the Extent of Role Model Obligations' (2012) 29 J Appl Philos 118, 118–23.

13 Feezell (n 12) 21.

14 See, e.g., *Trustees of the Barry Congregation of Jehovah's Witnesses v BXB* [2023] UKSC 15, [58] (Lord Burrows).

15 [2020] UKSC 13.

16 [2020] UKSC 12.

17 See *Lister v Hesley Hall Ltd* [2002] 1 AC 215, [60] (Lord Hobhouse).

18 CAS 2008/A/1605 *Jongewaard v Australian Olympic Committee*, [19].

19 Carole Epstein, 'Morals Clauses: Past, Present and Future' (2015) 5 J Intellect Prop Ent Law 72, 82.

20 Elle Madalin, 'Tolerance is Tricky Business: Israel Folau at the Court of Arbitration for Sport and the Moral Case for the Protection of Athletes' Free Expression' (2017) 12 ANZSLJ 53, 53.

21 Caysee Kamenetsky, 'The Need for Strict Morality Clauses in Endorsement Contracts' (2017) 7 Pace Intellect Prop Sport Ent Law Forum 289, 290.

22 Fernando Pinguelo and Timothy Cedrone, 'Morals? Who Cares About Morals? An Examination of Morals Clauses in Talent Contracts and What Talent Needs to Know' (2009) 19 Seton Hall J Sports & Ent L 347, 364.

23 Premier League, 'Handbook, Season 2020/21' <https://resources.premier-league.com/premierleague/document/2020/08/11/1256c4b9–23bb-4247–93c0–028f042b010d/2020–21-PL-Handbook-110820.pdf>, clause 3.2.5.

24 Rugby Football Union, 'Standard Form Player Contract – Version 2018' <https://www.englandrugby.com/dxdam/6a/6af05ffc-de18–42cf-8967–1ee2e688bd60/PremiershipStandardPlayerContract.pdf>, clause 6.8.

25 Rugby Football Union, 'Rules of the RFU' <https://www.englandrugby.com/dxdam/27/27533fb9-f2b8–429c-85d4-e190658d658d/2020–21%20Rules%20final.pdf>, clause 5.12.

26 Gerard Meagher, 'Danny Cipriani Avoids Ban as RFU Decides to Take No Further Action' (*The Guardian*, 23 August 2018) <https://www.theguardian.com/sport/2018/aug/22/danny-cipriani-avoids-ban-after-rfu-hearing>.

27 See, e.g., World Professional Billiards and Snooker Association, 'WPBSA Members Rules and Regulations' <https://wpbsa.com/wp-content/uploads/WPBSA-Members-Rules-as-amended-18.01.17.pdf>, clause 1.3.

28 [2008] EWCA Civ 689, [7].

29 For off-the-field harm caused by athletes in *individual* sports (who are by nature of their role not part of a club), the governing body alone will be the primary target for a vicarious liability claim. I consider this possibility in James Brown, 'The Vicarious Liability of Sports Governing Bodies and Competition Organisers' (2023) 43 LS 221.

30 James Brown, 'Vicarious Liability for On-Loan Sports Participants' (2022) 22 ISLR 40, 42–5.

31 Pinguelo and Cedrone (n 22) 351.

32 It is notable that, according to Simon Gardiner and others, *Sports Law* (4th edn, Routledge 2012) 395, 'in German law, a competition organiser or a sponsor could be considered an employer.'

33 Alexandra Topping, 'Sexual Misconduct Cases at Record High in Legal Profession' (*The Guardian*, 20 January 2020) <https://www.theguardian.com/law/2020/jan/20/sexual-misconduct-cases-at-record-high-in-legal-profession>.

34 See generally Kadence Otto, 'Criminal Athletes: An Analysis of Charges, Reduced Charges and Sentences' (2009) 19 JLAS 67.

35 Brown (n 29) 230–1.

36 [2016] UKSC 10, [22] (Lord Reed); [2017] UKSC 60, [55] (Lord Reed).

37 Andrew Zarriello, 'A Call to the Bullpen: Alternatives to the Morality Clause as Endorsement Companies' Main Protection against Athletic Scandal' (2015) 56 BCL Rev 389, 396; Sarah Katz, 'Reputations - A Lifetime to Build, Seconds to Destroy: Maximizing the Mutually Protective Value of Morals Clauses in Talent Agreements' (2011) 20 Cardozo J Int'l & Comp L 185, 190.

38 *Various Claimants v Catholic Child Welfare Society* [2012] UKSC 56, [35] (Lord Phillips).

39 *Cox v Ministry of Justice* [2016] UKSC 10, [23].

40 Murad Ahmed, 'Ronaldo: Why Juventus Gambled €100m on a Future Payday' (*Financial Times*, 16 September 2018) <https://www.ft.com/content/cc72b6a6-b5b9-11e8-b3ef-799c8613f4a1>. The former chairman Andrea Agnelli admitted that this transfer was 'the first time that the commercial side and the sporting side of Juventus came together in assessing the costs and benefits [of a signing].'

41 ibid.

42 Ben Hoyle, 'Nike 'Deeply Concerned' by Cristiano Ronaldo Rape Claim' (*The Times*, 05 October 2018) <https://www.thetimes.co.uk/article/nike-deeply-concerned-by-cristiano-ronaldo-rape-claim-b52drmdx8>.

43 John Duerden, 'Ronaldo's 90 Minutes on the Bench in Seoul was Another Own Goal in Asia' (*The Guardian*, 30 July 2019) <https://www.theguardian.com/football/2019/jul/30/cristiano-ronaldo-juventus-european-clubs-asia-tours>.

44 Ben Hoyle, 'Ronaldo Rape Allegations Wipe €100m off Value of Juventus' (*The Times*, 06 October 2018) <https://www.thetimes.co.uk/article/ronaldo-rape-allegations-wipe-100m-off-value-of-juventus-vr9vh3w3k>.

45 *CCWS* (n 38), [35].

46 In this light, and due to the relationship requirement at stage one, it would be Manchester United who would be held vicariously liable if the victim decided to commence a civil claim. Only if the rape occurred whilst Ronaldo was contracted to Juventus would the Italian club be held liable.

47 [2013] EWHC 2869 (QB).

48 ibid, [50]. See also Sarah Hook and Sandy Noakes, 'Employer Control of Employee Behaviour Through Social Media' (2019) 1 Law Technology & Humans 141, 156 (noting that there are 'some employees (e.g., Israel Folau) whose position and status within an organisation are such that it is clearly part of their employment contract to protect the employer's reputation at all times').

49 ibid [38].

50 See, e.g., Premier League (n 23), clause 4; Martin Kosla, 'Disciplined for Bringing a Sport into Disrepute – A Framework for Judicial Review' (2001) 25 MULR 654, 673.

51 [2015] EWHC 2862 (QB), [148] (HHJ Butler).

52 Andrew Bell 'The Liability of Local Authorities for Abuses by Foster Parents' (2018) 34 PN 38, 41.

53 Robert Flannigan, 'Enterprise Control: The Servant-Independent Contractor Distinction' (1987) 37 UTLJ 25, 33 (noting that 'a person's ability to benefit in an equity or residual sense normally depends on whether or not that person controls the performance of the work').

54 Paul Jonson, Sandra Lynch and Daryl Adair, 'The Contractual and Ethical Duty for a Professional Athlete to be an Exemplary Role Model: Bringing the Sport and Sportsperson into Unreasonable and Unfair Disrepute' (2013) 8 ANZSLJ 55, 59.

55 Kosla (n 50) 655; Jason Haynes, 'Social Justice Movements and the Neutrality of Sport: The Case for Re-Defining the "No Disrepute" Clause' (2021) 1 ISLR 4, 6–7.
56 CAS 2008/A/1574, [46]. See also CAS 2007/A/1291 *Zubkov v FINA*, [20].
57 CAS OG 16/009 *Russian Weightlifting Federation (RWF) v International Weightlifting Federation (IWF)*, [7.13].
58 As evidenced in *Jongewaard* (n 18), [18], the appellant had a 'contractual obligation to not engage in (publicly known) conduct which, *in the absolute discretion of the President of the AOC*, brought or would be likely to bring him into disrepute.' [emphasis added].
59 [1970] AC 1004, 1055.
60 John Davidson, 'Reconciling the Tension between Employer Liability and Employee Privacy' (1998) 8 Geo Mason U Civ Rts LJ 145, 147–8.
61 James Paterson, 'Disciplining Athletes for Off-Field Indiscretions: A Comparative Review of the Australian Football League and the National Football League's Personal Conduct Policies' (2009) 4 ANZSLJ 105, 136.
62 [2016] UKSC 11, [45].
63 *Lister* (n 17), [83] (Lord Millett referring to an 'inherent' risk); *Brayshaw v Partners of Apsley Surgery* [2018] EWHC 3286 (QB), [69] (Spencer J referring to a 'reasonably incidental' risk).
64 *Fairchild v Glenhaven Funeral Services Ltd* [2002] UKHL 22; *Sienkiewicz v Greif (UK) Ltd* [2011] UKSC 10.
65 See text to Chapter 4, n 77.
66 Craig Jenkins and Tom Ellis, 'The Highway to Hooliganism - An Evaluation of the Impact of Combat Sport Participation on Individual Criminality' (2011) 13 Int J Police Sci Manag 117, 120; Michael Flood and Sue Dyson, 'Sport, Athletes, and Violence Against Women' (2007) 4 NTV Journal 37, 38; David Whitson, 'The Embodiment of Gender: Discipline, Domination and Empowerment' in Susan Birrell and Cheryl Cole (eds), *Women, Sport, and Culture* (Human Kinetics 1994) 367.
67 Wendy MacGregor, 'It's Just a Game Until Someone Is Sexually Assaulted: Sport Culture and the Perpetuation of Sexual Violence by Athletes' (2018) 28 Educ Law J 43, 51.
68 Gordon Forbes et al., 'Aggressive High School Sports Attitudes Among College Men as a Function of Participation in Dating Aggression, Sexual Coercion, and Aggression-Supporting' (2006) 12 Violence Against Women 441, 450–1.
69 Deborah Brake, 'Sport and Masculinity: The Promise and Limits of Title IX' in Frank Cooper and Ann McGinley (eds), *Masculinities and the Law: A Multidimensional Approach* (NYU Press 2012) 211.
70 Scot Boeringer, 'Associations of Rape-Supportive Attitudes with Fraternal and Athletic Participation' (1999) 5 Violence Against Women 81.
71 Elizabeth Gage, 'Gender Attitudes and Sexual Behaviors: Comparing Center and Marginal Athletes and Nonathletes in a Collegiate Setting' (2008) 14 Violence Against Women 1014.
72 Michael Welch, 'Violence Against Women by Professional Football Players: A Gender Analysis of Hypermasculinity, Positional Status, Narcissism, and Entitlement' (1997) 21 J Sport Soc Issues 392.
73 See, e.g., Samuele Zilioli and Neil Watson, 'Testosterone Across Successive Competitions: Evidence for a 'Winner Effect' in Humans?' (2014) 47 Psychoneuroendocrinology 1.
74 Esperanza Gonzalez-Bono et al., 'Testosterone, Cortisol, and Mood in a Sports Team Competition' (1999) 35 Horm Behav 55.
75 ibid 61 (noting that forwards in a professional basketball game in Spain had higher increases in testosterone levels than centers and guards).
76 398 F 2d 167, p.172 (2d Cir. 1968).

77 Wanda Leal, Marc Gertz and Alex Piquero, 'The National Felon League?': A Comparison of NFL Arrests to General Population Arrests' (2015) 43 J Crim Just 397, 400. Notably, NFL players also had a substantially lower arrest rate for property crimes, such as burglary, theft and fraud.

78 BBC, 'Henry Ruggs III: NFL Star Faces Charges over Fatal Drink-Driving Crash' (*BBC News*, 03 November 2021) <https://www.bbc.co.uk/news/world-us-canada-59143625>. See also Jon Bois, 'Are Pro Athletes More Likely to Get Arrested for DUI?' (*SB Nation*, 06 June 2012) <https://www.sbnation.com/nfl/2012/6/6/3066024/justin-blackmon-pro-athlete-dui>.

79 Warren Fiske, 'Vick Pleads Guilty, Apologizes in Dogfighting Case' (*Reuters*, 27 August 2007) <https://www.reuters.com/article/us-nfl-vick-idUSN2744252420070827>.

80 Leal, Gertz and Piquero (n 77) 400 (noting that 2004 was the only year in which the violent crime arrest rate was higher for the general population than for NFL athletes. In other years – such as 2007 and 2008 – the arrest rate for violent crime amongst NFL players was more than double that of the general population).

81 [2002] EMLR 22, [60].

82 *PJS v News Group Newspapers Ltd* [2016] UKSC 26, [32] (Lord Mance).

6 Conclusion

This book has sought to explore the appropriate scope of the close connection test for vicarious liability in the sports industry. It is the first work to provide an in-depth and up-to-date application of vicarious liability for several torts in a multitude of different sports. The book adopts a theoretical approach that is informed by several of the leading justifications for the doctrine: enterprise liability (in both its benefit and risk forms), control, loss spreading, deep pockets, and deterrence. In recognising that enterprise liability is likely to be the strongest justification in most contexts, Chapter 2 outlined that courts ought to empirically assess the inherent risks of each sport so as to avoid a clash with an assessment of a sport's playing culture at the standard of care stage. Thereafter, Chapter 3 argued for the introduction of a (potentially sport-specific) tort of hate speech to respond to racial slurs used on the field. Again, a risk-based approach, informed by insights from Critical Race Theory, was employed here in order to highlight the institutionally racist nature of many sports clubs.

The book also recognised, however, that vicarious liability is not just strictly limited to on-the-field acts. Chapter 4 considered that enterprise liability could equally be utilised to hold clubs vicariously liable for a wide range of off-the-field acts too. In particular, it argued that several sexual offences – such as hazing rookie athletes and sexually assaulting women – could be found to be closely connected to one's employment as a professional athlete. This was reinforced in Chapter 5, where it was highlighted that a fairness-based approach (predicated on the ubiquity of pervasive disrepute clauses) could also support the imposition of vicarious liability for off-the-field acts. The book concluded by offering several guiding factors that judges may wish to consider when applying vicarious liability for acts committed away from the field.

In making these arguments, the book has highlighted several important broader lessons that can be learnt about vicarious liability by applying it to the sports industry. For instance, the application to sport in this book appears to demonstrate that a more sustained theoretical approach to vicarious liability is desirable. Whilst the pendulum seems to have now swung back to a

DOI: 10.4324/9781032665870-6

more restrictive model of vicarious liability following *Barclays Bank v Various Claimants*[1] and *WM Morrison Supermarkets v Various Claimants*,[2] the book argues that a detailed application of theory may lead to better results in practice. One example of this can be seen in Chapter 5. There, I discussed *GB v Stoke City Football Club Ltd*,[3] a case in which the presiding judge ruled out liability for the alleged off-the-field abuse of a young professional footballer. However, it was demonstrated how the adoption of a risk-based approach in that case might have produced a more normatively and empirically desirable outcome on the facts.

Of course, the theoretical approach advocated in this book is likely to lead to a wider scope of liability than that envisioned by the Supreme Court in *Barclays* and *Morrison*, but this would not necessarily lead to overly broad liability. In fact, an application of the underlying rationales for vicarious liability may help to rein in widespread liability in some contexts. This was evidenced most clearly by my rejection of a role model-based test in relation to vicarious liability for off-the-field acts.[4] It was suggested in Chapter 5 that this approach, which had seemingly been implicitly supported by some scholars, would lead to an overly extensive scope of vicarious liability in this context. As such, even those in favour of the narrow approach in *Barclays* and *Morrison* may still accept some of the findings made in this book.

A sport-specific application of vicarious liability was also useful in demonstrating that the doctrine ought to be sensitive to insight from other socio-legal interdisciplinary fields. It was maintained that such insight could help to enrich some of the traditional rationales for vicarious liability. This was evidenced, for instance, by considering how Critical Race Theory could inform a risk-based approach to liability for on-the-field discrimination (in Chapter 3). Likewise, the broader field of gender studies was utilised (in Chapters 4 and 5) to illustrate how both masculinities studies and feminist theory might intellectually enhance an enterprise liability analysis of off-the-field acts. The suggestion that other (less conventional) theories could inform the more traditional rationales for vicarious liability may go some way to striking an appropriate balance between the law's need to both respect tradition and make progress. A recognition of this inherent tension within the law once again reinforces the legal realist school of thought that underpins much of the analysis in this book.

Relatedly, legal realist scholars also tend to stress the importance of empirical studies to substantiate normative claims, and the sport-specific analysis in this book has demonstrated the need to refer to empirical data when applying the close connection test. This was evidenced most clearly in Chapter 4, and it was suggested there that a material contribution-based test may need to be adopted in cases where we are unable to precisely pinpoint the specific causes of a particular risk. Aside from this, Chapter 2 also demonstrated the significance of adopting an empirical approach to vicarious liability. There, I argued that an empirical analysis of risk ought to be adopted for the purposes of vicarious liability, but a normative standard when assessing risk at the standard of care stage. This solution to the so-called 'double-edged sword' problem could be justified by explicitly recognising the different policy bases that underpin these two disparate areas of law.

As we can see, then, the book often calls for result-oriented solutions and it tends to view law in 'functional terms' as a means to an end.[5] This is demonstrated not only by the empirical-normative dichotomy outlined in Chapter 2 but also by other suggested developments that were outlined in later chapters. For example, the argument for introducing a new tort of hate speech in Chapter 3 was primarily based around the fact that vicarious liability (and indeed tort law more broadly) currently struggles to effectively respond to discriminatory behaviour. Now, I have no problem in admitting that some of the recommendations made in this book are unorthodox, but sometimes difficult problems call for unique solutions.

A further theme that emerges from the analysis in this book relates to the interplay between many of the theoretical justifications for vicarious liability. The application of these rationales to sport highlighted that certain theories may be afforded more weight in certain contexts. For instance, Chapter 2 highlighted that enterprise risk appears to be a stronger consideration than deterrence and benefit enterprise liability in the context of on-the-field personal injuries. This was a point that was seemingly overlooked by Clarke MR in his leading judgment in *Gravil v Carroll and Redruth Rugby Football Club*.[6]

In other contexts, it may not be a case of identifying which theory provides the strongest indication of liability but rather whether certain theories can work together to produce a desirable outcome. In Chapter 5, for instance, it was observed that both risk and benefit may need to work together harmoniously if vicarious liability is to be justified for any off-the-field harm that does not contribute to the positive reputation of an employer. Nevertheless, the fact that many of the theories seem to overlap – as evidenced by the similarities between benefit and control in Chapter 5 – may make it slightly easier to identify some degree of harmony between many of these rationales. With this in mind, it is suggested that the discussion in this book has contributed not only to the broader theoretical debates in vicarious liability, tort law and private law but also to the emerging field of sports law. In particular, it is hoped that an application of these private law theories to the sporting context may provide a number of important pragmatic and conceptual benefits to the growing area of 'sports torts'.

Of course, however, whilst the book strives to make a number of important theoretical, socio-legal and jurisprudential contributions, it would be remiss to downplay some of the other significant conclusions made in this work. From a doctrinal point of view, for instance, an application of vicarious liability to the sports sector exemplified the need to dispose of the unhelpful distinction between negligent and intentional acts in determining the closeness of connection in each case. As illustrated in Chapter 2, this negligent-intentional divide seems to be out of step with recent case law developments which illustrate that employers can be held vicariously liable for deliberately inflicted injury. Similarly, a sport-specific analysis of the doctrine in Chapter 5 revealed that it may be permissible to draw on cases in closely related areas of law – such as unfair dismissal and privacy – to provide an instructive steer for the application of the close connection test in relation to extramural activity. This reference to other areas of law perhaps further reinforces the contention that the underlying focus of this book is on *what* the purpose of law is and *how* judges ought to apply it.

Additionally, and from a practical point of view, it is worth noting that much of the discussion in this book may be of interest to practitioners, policymakers and various stakeholders in sport (such as sports clubs, governing bodies, competition organisers, sponsors and athletes). For instance, judges may wish to consult the six-point guidance offered in Chapter 5 when applying the doctrine of vicarious liability for off-the-field conduct. This guidance once again reinforces the heavily contextualised and fact-sensitive nature of my suggested model of liability, particularly as it was maintained that such guidance ought to be applied using a spectrum-based approach. Likewise, the analysis in Chapter 2 also illustrated that other legal practitioners, such as barristers, may wish to consider presenting some form of empirical evidence to support a risk-based claim when dealing with on-the-field personal injury.

Sports clubs may also be interested in the arguments presented in this book. Indeed, the analysis here indicates that it may be useful to draw an important distinction between amateur clubs and professional clubs when applying the close connection test at stage two. Chapter 2 highlighted that professional clubs are more likely to be found vicariously liable for on-the-field personal injury, as it was observed that such clubs are more likely to attain some financial and/or sporting benefit from violent on-the-field behaviour by one of their players. It was also argued there that the fairness rationale ought to be subject to an important clarification: just because an employer suffers loss from a particular activity does not necessarily mean that they do not also benefit from it. Likewise, Chapter 3 illustrated that professional clubs may also be more susceptible to vicarious liability for on-field discrimination too, as it was contended that the highly visible nature of this behaviour arguably makes it more culpable (and thus deserving of a stronger legal response).

The contention that professional clubs are more likely to be held vicariously liable for harmful behaviour is equally true for off-the-field conduct as well. As demonstrated in Chapters 4 and 5, the fact that amateur sportsmen are not celebrities means that the blurred line between on-duty and off-duty conduct is not particularly relevant for recreational athletes. Consequently, whilst I have argued elsewhere that amateur athletes could potentially satisfy the stage one (relationship) test of vicarious liability,[7] recreational sports clubs may take some comfort in the fact that it appears to be more difficult to satisfy the close connection test in the amateur sports context.

Aside from this amateur/professional distinction, other practical implications of the analysis in this book include: the need to eliminate (or at least modify the scope of) overly extensive and intrusive disrepute clauses (Chapter 5); the potential for governing bodies, competition organisers and sponsors to be held dually vicariously liable for off-the-field conduct (Chapter 5); and the fact that injured players – and indeed defendant clubs – may wish to opt for a vicarious liability claim (rather than an action in negligence) when seeking damages from an employer for on-the-field harm. This latter point was demonstrated when discussing the *suitability argument* in Chapter 2. Indeed, a club held vicariously liable for an intentional on-the-field act will usually be able to rely on their insurers to foot the bill. This is not typically the case for primary liability claims. As such, from a practical (and loss spreading) perspective, it may be preferable for claimants to pursue an action in vicarious liability for such harm.

Finally, it must be noted that, whilst the book touches upon some lasting debates in both sports law and private/tort law, it is impossible to cover every single issue that might be raised when discussing the close connection test in the sports industry. However, it is hoped that the analysis in this book could lead to several interesting lines of enquiry for further research.

First, it would be interesting to assess the scope of the close connection test for wrongs committed by athletes on social media (which would, it is suggested, also be informed by a fairness-based approach predicated on the use of disrepute clauses). Second, it may be useful to assess whether a sports employer held vicariously liable ought to have a right of indemnification against their wrongdoing employee. Whilst the use of indemnities is not practically feasible in most employment contexts (given the shallow pockets of most tortfeasors),[8] we must remember that, in professional sport at least, many athletes are highly paid and expensively acquired employees. In this regard, the sporting context is rather unique, and it may thus be reasonable for the wrongdoing athlete to indemnify their club for any on-the-field or off-the-field loss they have caused.

Support for this proposition might be gleaned from the lengthy legal proceedings involving the former professional footballer Adrian Mutu, who was ordered to pay £15.2m in damages to his former employer, Chelsea FC, after unilaterally breaching his contractual obligations.[9] Although the club's case against Mutu centred around his unlawful ingestion of cocaine (which led to a seven-month ban from the sport, and his subsequent dismissal from Chelsea FC), similar reasoning could be equally applicable to any breach of contract resulting from an athlete's tortious behaviour.[10] Whether the acceptance of an indemnity in professional sport is inconsistent with employer-employee relations – a factor that militates against the existence of an indemnification claim in most other industries[11] – is also interesting in light of the fact that contracts and relationships routinely break down in this context (usually after a player has handed in a transfer request).

The third avenue for future research relates to the possibility of conducting empirical studies to further support some of the normative and theoretical arguments made in this book. This could include, for instance, empirical research into whether the imposition of vicarious liability on sports clubs actually deters foul play (as was suggested in *Gravil*). As was mentioned in Chapter 2 when discussing the *practicality argument*, it may not be wise to rely on deterrence in the absence of empirical evidence. Similarly, empirical analysis exploring the prevalence of hazing and sexual abuse in professional UK sport would also be a useful line of enquiry.

The fourth (and most broad) recommendation for future work was touched upon in the introduction, and it concerns the potential scope of vicarious liability for other individuals in the sporting industry, such as managers, coaches, scouts, nutritionists and medical staff. It is hoped that the in-depth discussion of the close connection test in this book could potentially lead to a more theoretical examination of vicarious liability for these other actors. Given my previous work on doping in sport,[12] it might be fruitful, for instance, to examine the potential vicarious liability of clubs for backroom staff who encourage their athletes to consume an illicit substance.[13]

Having outlined the potential avenues for future research on this topic, it is perhaps instructive to end this book where we began: with the comments of the legendary American football coach, Vince Lombardi. In one of his most famous quotes, he suggested that '[p]erfection is not attainable, but if we chase perfection we can catch excellence'.[14] In a similar vein, and in light of the potential uncertainty generated by my suggested recommendations, it would be overly presumptuous to maintain that the arguments formulated in this book will lead to a perfect law on vicarious liability. After all, the vast judicial discretion that is created by my model of vicarious liability is likely to remain a significant issue for those who espouse a more principled, incremental approach. However, by at least striving for perfection – that is to say, by adopting a theoretical and interdisciplinary conception of the doctrine that is sensitive to the wide array of contexts, factual scenarios and empirical studies that may all influence the outcome of a case – we may be able to achieve an excellent law on vicarious liability. And in light of the vast doctrinal inconsistencies and theoretical uncertainties that have plagued this area of law for well over a century, excellence is, I believe, more than sufficient.

Notes

1 [2020] UKSC 13.
2 [2020] UKSC 12.
3 [2015] EWHC 2862 (QB).
4 Additionally, it may also be evidenced by the fact that the analysis in Chapters 4 and 5 would not automatically apply to other famous tortfeasors (as it was suggested that there are important differences between sport and other industries).
5 Randall Kelso, 'Separation of Powers Doctrine on the Modern Supreme Court and Four Doctrinal Approaches to Judicial Decision-Making' (1993) 20 Pepp L Rev 531, 537–8.

6 [2008] EWCA Civ 689.

7 James Brown, 'Vicarious Liability in Amateur Sport: The Problem with Unincorporated Associations' (LawInSport, 29 June 2023).

8 Paula Giliker, *Vicarious Liability in Tort: A Comparative Perspective* (CUP 2010) 31; *London Drugs Ltd v Kuehne & Nagel International Ltd* (1993) 97 DLR (4th) 261, 284 (La Forest J).

9 For the latest instalment in this saga – which involved the European Court of Human Rights upholding the award against Mutu – see *Mutu and Pechstein v Switzerland*, App nos 40575/10 and 67474/10 (ECtHR, 2 October 2018).

10 For a non-sporting example, see *Lister v Romford Ice and Cold Storage* [1957] AC 555 (employer held vicariously liable for the negligent actions of their employee lorry driver, but the defendants were able to successfully claim back £1600 in damages from the wrongdoer himself).

11 See, e.g., *Morris v Ford Motor Co. Ltd* [1973] 1 QB 792, 798 (Lord Denning MR).

12 James Brown, 'Genetic Doping: WADA we do About the Future of 'Cheating' in Sport?' (2019) 19 ISLJ 258.

13 See, e.g., Australian Associated Press, 'Cronulla Sharks Face Legal Action from Third Former Player over Supplements' (*The Guardian*, 05 February 2014) <https://www.theguardian.com/sport/2014/feb/06/cronulla-sharks-legal-supplements-broderick-wright>; Mark Russell, 'Former Essendon Rookie Hal Hunter to Sue Club over Supplements Program' (*The Age*, 10 February 2016) <https://www.theage.com.au/national/victoria/former-essendon-rookie-hal-hunter-to-sue-club-over-supplements-program-20160210-gmqeea.html>. This possibility was also touched upon by Joellen Riley and David Weiler, 'Modern-Day Gladiators: The Professional Athlete Employment Relationship Under the World Anti-Doping Code' in Ulrich Haas and Deborah Healey (eds), *Doping in Sport and the Law* (Hart 2016) 179–80.

14 Family of Vince Lombardi c/o Luminary Group, 'Famous Quotes by Vince Lombardi' <http://www.vincelombardi.com/quotes.html>.

Index

For Product Safety Concerns and Information please contact our EU
representative GPSR@taylorandfrancis.com
Taylor & Francis Verlag GmbH, Kaufingerstraße 24, 80331 München, Germany

9 781032 665863